Finding Joy in the Life You've
Never Imagined Through God's
Grace

AUTHENTICALLY ANCHORED

SHONDA RAMSEY

Authentically Anchored
Published by Authentically Created
PO Box 532
Springboro, Ohio 45066
www.authenticallycreated.com

Authentically Created is a division of Lilian Grace Designs, LLC

ISBN 979-8-9898545-0-9 (paperback)
eISBN 979-8-9898545-1-6 (epub)

Library of Congress Control Number: 2024909161

Cover design and photograph by Shonda Ramsey

Printed in the United States of America
First Edition 2024

10 9 8 7 6 5 4 3 2 1

080324

Authentically
CREATED

Endorsements

"Shonda Ramsey's *Authentically Anchored* is a moving exploration of womanhood, resilience, and identity. Through heartfelt reflections, Shonda explores the vulnerable journey of rebuilding shattered dreams. Her ability to infuse authenticity and raw emotion into every page makes this novel a powerful testament to both the resilience of the human spirit and God's healing power. *Authentically Anchored* is a captivating narrative that will leave readers with the tools, strength, and know-how to move forward in Christ."

—Amber Parr Burdett,
Editor, Author, and Writing Coach

"In *Authentically Anchored*, Shonda Ramsey extends a compassionate hand to those engulfed by life's storms. Her book, brimming with sincerity and raw honesty, serves as a morning beacon of hope and healing. It's like sitting down with a wise friend who knows your pain and guides you toward hope with gentle words and profound understanding."

—Krissy Nelson
Author, Speaker, Coach
Krissy Nelson Consulting

"Whether you're struggling with unfulfilled dreams, a loss of identity, or seeking clarity in your life's direction, *Authentically Anchored* offers you a lifeline. Through personal storytelling, wisdom from scripture, thought-provoking questions, and engaging journal prompts, Shonda Ramsey comes alongside to guide you toward the shore of a more authentic and fulfilled life."

—Rebecca Madden
Co-author of *Breathless Haste: Finding God in Ordinary Life*

"*Authentically Anchored* shows the journey we often find ourselves in, from drifting at sea to firm in the hands of the One who created it. Through her personal experiences, Shonda Ramsey shows us that while our stories may differ, hope overcomes the overwhelm and hopelessness. Imagine if we each looked into the mirror and spoke life, as we see her do time and again throughout the book. What a powerful practice!"

—Tami Kennimer Gray
Author of *Fearlessly Unbecoming*
Virtual Assistant to Authors & Entrepreneurs
Tattooed Wedding Rings and Whiskey Prayers

"In her book *Authentically Anchored*, Shonda Ramsey vulnerably shares various seasons of her life, offering invaluable lessons learned through them. She gives tangible tools to help you on your own journey with God through disappointments and discouragement, helping you uncover His plans for your life. You'll feel like a friend is in your corner helping you step into who you were created to be."

—Jenn Schultz
Author of *She's Not Your Enemy*

"Through reading Shonda Ramsey's *Authentically Anchored,* you learn not to rely on your own strength to go through life's trials. Things in life, such as labels others place on you, can ultimately weigh you down. But when you focus on what God says, you discover your true authentic self.

Open the door to life's challenges by stepping into His boldness and gain the confidence you need by saying yes to the challenge. As you read this book, you will use these newly discovered parts of your authentic self and God's grace to live abundantly in the highs and lows of life. "

—Paula Villarreal
Author of *Dream Again*

To my husband, Mike.

Thank you for choosing to love me even on my darkest days. You have always picked up the pieces of my broken heart and rearranged them in a way that exudes beauty. Your loving patience, as I searched high and low to discover my identity, helped me see who I was in your eyes. I am forever grateful to be growing old with you and will cherish every memory we make together. You are my family.

Disclaimer

This book was written with the Christian faith in mind, referencing verses from the Holy Bible and making mention of God, Father, Jesus, Lord, and Holy Spirit. I recognize there are many different religious beliefs; if your faith is different from Christianity, I encourage you to read my book with an open mind and apply your faith where applicable. It is important to note that I am an imperfect Christian, but I am always seeking to learn, to do, and to be better. The contents of this book are straight from my heart. It is my hope that you'll find comfort in the scriptures and companionship in the pages that lie before you.

Contents

Introduction

I found myself adrift, searching for an anchor to steady my soul. The more I tried to be someone I wasn't, the farther I drifted out to sea, searching for a way to anchor my identity amid changing tides. The ocean in its magnitude is beautiful to look at, with moody waves that rise and crash down, creating a landscape of soft peaks and swirls of light mixing in with the water. How can something so beautiful on the surface carry such darkness below that threatens to extinguish lives?

Another life-altering discovery came as I found myself at the bottom of the ocean. It felt as if God, Himself, had betrayed me, all hope was lost, and there was nothing more I could do except give up. I had become unrecognizable as I settled in on the ocean bed, wrapped tightly by the anchor's chain that held me in place, each link adorned with its tiny little labels of words that defined me.

Have you ever felt the weight of your identity slipping through your fingers as the world redefines who you are by assigning labels to you? The overwhelming feeling of failure from being misunderstood and incorrectly labeled adds to the weight of the chain. This wasn't how I wanted my life to go, and if I'm being completely honest with myself, I didn't know if I wanted the life that lay before me. I had no control over my circumstances, and though I knew I should trust God's big plan for my life, there was zero chance of me believing that any of this could be for the greater good despite knowing God's truth.

During my time spent in the depths of despair, I lived life on autopilot—not feeling or experiencing life in the way it was meant to be. The pressure of the waves above and around me was so massive that I couldn't escape because it, along with the anchor, felt so heavy. Have you ever felt as if you were in a cold, dark place, with no one around you, unable to move or escape? It is there, at the bottom of the ocean, that you find yourself held captive by believing the many lies told by the enemy who tries his hardest to destroy you. You wrestle with your thoughts and ideas of the different ways you failed or didn't measure up, and you remember all the people who rejected you or told you that you weren't enough.

Like most people, I had many hopes and dreams. I even daydreamed about a life that I hoped to one day have, only to find myself living a reality far from what I envisioned. I had lost my identity, and my faith in God also began to waver. I longed to discover who I was in this new season. I knew I needed to strip everything back, but starting over felt like an impossible thing to do.

Perhaps your story is like mine, in that you have found yourself living a life you've never imagined. Circumstances beyond your control may have been the driving force that tossed you into the ocean where you feel alone and unsure of what to do next. The grief and guilt you carry keep you captive in the cold murky waters. Grief over the loss of love, friendship, a job, a child, a parent, or a dream. Guilt over the choices you've made in your past, the things you did or didn't say, how you acted, not doing the right thing, or even doing the right thing.

What if I told you there is a way to escape the bottom of the ocean and find yourself authentically anchored in Christ on the shore, unable to be thrown back in? Finding joy in the life I've never imagined has been challenging, but through God's grace, He opened my eyes to an infinite number of possibilities that await me. I only had to act and reach the shore. I invite you to join me as you rediscover who you are, where together we take action to help you reach the shore too.

Personal Retreat of Rediscovery

I wrote this book as a personal retreat of rediscovery. I encourage you to take your time in each chapter, completing all the steps at the end before you advance in the book. One chapter could take you an hour or a year, the choice is yours to make, but it is important to not skip through chapters or you may miss an important step that could alter your outcome.

Each chapter offers a valuable life lesson, giving you the chance to get to know me and my process of rediscovering my identity. It is in these life lessons I share my most vulnerable states, some of which I have never shared with anyone before.

As I share my journey through a season of rebuilding after loss, I hope you'll see me not just as a guide but as a fellow traveler on this path. By sharing my own vulnerabilities, I hope to bridge the gap between us, making this more than just words on a page. It's my sincerest wish that as you turn these pages, you feel a sense of companionship, knowing you're not navigating this season alone. Consider me not just an author but a friend in your corner, rooting for you every step of the way.

What you can expect at the end of each chapter

Identity Struggle – The thing that threatens to steal our identity in God. I leave you with a question to get you thinking about your life and how my life lesson can be applied. I encourage you to write it in your journal and add your response to the question when you feel you are ready.

Glimpses of Grace – Where we can find God's grace in His word and apply it to our lives. I recount stories from the Bible that helped me work through my valuable life lesson and show you where grace can be found.

The Heart of the Matter – What this means in our current moment. I take my valuable life lesson and teach you how to navigate similar situations. I encourage you to think of one situation in your life that closely resembles mine and see if the lesson can be applied.

Finding Joy – How or where you can find joy in all of it. I know that when you first start reading, finding joy may feel like something that is not easily attainable. When I was in the bottom of the ocean, there was no joy visible, but with action, joy became evident.

Anchor Points – Actionable steps you can take to uncover who you are after going through hardships and give you the end goal of rebranding your life.

Scripture Memorization – Rooting yourself in God's word is the necessary foundation for rediscovering your identity. Philippians 4:13, *"I can do all this through him who gives me strength."*

Prayer – Inviting Jesus to have a personal encounter with you. Psalms 107:1–3, *"Give thanks to the Lord, for he is good; his love endures forever. Let the redeemed of the Lord tell their story—those he redeemed from the hand of the foe, those he gathered from the lands, from east and west, from north and south."*

Journal Prompts – Your promise to God that you are all in on being authentically anchored in Him.

Declaration Statements – Taking ownership of who you are in this season and who you hope to be at the end of this book.

Resources to Have on Hand

This book is an interactive book, with encouragement to act on rediscovering your identity. There are resources listed here that I personally use daily and will help you maximize your experience. I recommend you gather as many of these items as possible and put them in a tote bag or some other small mobile container so you can take them with you wherever you choose to do the activities mentioned in this book. I call this my growth bag.

Growth Bag Contents:
- Authentically Anchored Book and Companion Workbook (optional, but recommended)

- Pocket or digital Bible
  - YouVersion App (or other similar)
- Journal
- Pens
- Paper (loose)
- Colored pencils, markers, or crayons
- Mirror
- Sticky notes or a dry erase marker
- Spotify Playlist

A Curated Spotify Playlist that coordinates with *Authentically Anchored*

A glimpse into the Companion Workbook

All that stands between you and rediscovering your identity is an open heart and mind. I ask that you give yourself grace and patience as you work through some difficult exercises to get to the root of who you are and rebuild your relationship with God.

Friend, I know you are hurting. You may be scared and alone in the darkness, longing for a hand to reach out and pull you to the surface. I know because I'm here beside you at the bottom of the ocean. You aren't alone; God wants you to know that He loves you and cares for you. Despite your broken moments, there is the possibility of finding joy in the life you've never imagined through God's grace and your resilience.

I hope that by sharing with you my innermost thoughts and fears, you will come to know and understand that while I may not be able to fully understand your situation, I can empathize. Will you join me as we swim to shore where I will weep with you, pray with you, and encourage you along the way?

Dedication

I, _____ , commit to not only reading 'Authentically Anchored' but also promise to open my heart as I engage with and apply the journal prompts and exercises provided at the end of each chapter as I begin to rebrand my life.

Signed,   Date: _____

Chapter One
Grace in Deep Waters

After enduring a series of traumatic life events, I found myself adrift—having lost my core sense of identity. I no longer recognized the woman in the mirror as my own reflection, so I stopped looking at her altogether. I disliked the person I had become—a shell of who I once was. My face was marked by the visible signs of sadness, anger, hatred, and even depression.

As a result, I abandoned all my hobbies, hopes, and dreams by settling into a detached life of isolation. The once extroverted person I was, was replaced with an introverted version of myself who preferred to struggle alone, pushing away those who even dared to reach out to me. My mind and heart had grown so dark I worried others would not like who I had become. Eventually, my fear was validated as one by one people distanced themselves, leaving me to wallow in my own misery.

The joy that once shone through me was replaced with despair as I settled firmly in my grief, unwilling to turn around and face God. I convinced myself it was easier to neglect my own well-being than it was to do the hard work of repairing the heartache. Looking back, I can see this was a lie straight from the enemy since giving up on myself only made my situation worse. It wasn't until I forced myself to look in the mirror again that I realized the woman staring back needed me to persevere—to be strong and keep going. *But how...*

It Started with a Dream

My dream of motherhood began with a dollhouse. When I was younger, I had an amazing dollhouse that came complete with furnishings to match the home that I grew up in—everything from the tile, carpet, and wallpaper, to a coo-coo clock that resembled the one in our living room, and even the porcelain bath fixtures. The amount of love that my parents put into the making of this dollhouse is something that brings me joy today, even though as a child I may not have realized just how much effort went into this treasured gift.

I would play with that dollhouse every day. With my little dolls designed to fit within the walls of the house, I would play "family" and act out a life that I one day hoped to have. The two-story home with black shutters and a black front door held inside the love of a man and woman with their three children and a fluffy dog. It never struck me that the dream family life I envisioned and enacted with such care might, in fact, never become my reality.

But, I was confronted with the distressing reality that having children would be difficult for me at the age of sixteen, after having gone to the doctor for a series of issues that came up due to me being a late bloomer and struggling with my weight. I was too young to fully process the magnitude of what this meant. I was scared and unsure of how to feel, but I was certain that I wanted to be a mom someday. I wrapped myself up in a cozy quilt as I cried myself to sleep that night and questioned the reason why I had to be faced with adversity while I mourned the thought of a life without children. This revelation immediately cast a shadow over me, evolving into a relentless source of worry and burden from that moment onwards. Infertility was something I hadn't ever heard of, let alone something I ever dreamed I would battle myself.

I tried not to put much thought into it again until infertility reared its ugly head in my early twenties during my first marriage as I went through fertility treatments. As the medication's side effects intensified, each day felt like a battle against time as I stared at yet another negative pregnancy test. The weight of disappointment pressed down on me. Hope slipped through my fingers like sand as I sat alone in the bathroom, the tiles cold against my skin and tears streaming down my cheeks as reality sunk in. The stress of the process began to add more and more pressure on us both, and eventually, the distance between us grew causing irreparable damage to our relationship. We fell out of love on our quest to become parents, which resulted in further disappointment and shattered dreams as the marriage came to an end.

It wasn't until five years later when I met Mike that I looked at my infertility as an opportunity and began to think about family outside of the normal ways most people have a family. When Mike and I started dating, I was honest with him from the very beginning and I shared with him that I couldn't have children. To my surprise, despite this news, he still chose to love me, and in his embrace, my heart overflowed with joy as a sense of belonging emerged. Early on, we decided that our life would look unique in comparison to most couples, and we were both perfectly okay with that since it took the pressure off the expectation of conceiving a child. We got married, bought a house with black shutters and a black front door, and we felt hopeful as we ventured down the long winding road of obtaining foster care licensing.

My dream evolved into the fairytale of holding a newborn baby whose family couldn't care for them and vowing to be the one there for the rest of that child's life. All I could do was fixate on the possibility of having a baby in the house as I stocked up a nursery full of diapers, clothing, and even a crib borrowed from family. As I stood in the nursery, the sunlight poured in through the window casting a warm glow on the changing table, and in that moment, I surrendered my heart to the hopeful possibility of finally becoming a mom and fulfilling my lifelong dream inside of my dream home.

Midway through the licensing process, something shifted in both of our hearts as the social workers shared a video with us that talked about the older children in foster care whom no one gave a chance. The video left me feeling like someone had punched me in the gut so hard that all of the air escaped me as a million thoughts ran through my mind. I'll never forget the moment when everything changed. We had just parked the car outside the restaurant where we were planning to have dinner, yet we found ourselves unable to leave the vehicle. As I sat there, reflections from the parenting class we had just attended overwhelmed me, and before I knew it, I was overrun with tears.

I shared with Mike that I felt called to help the older children because I felt they needed us more. I feared he would be disappointed that we wouldn't get to hold a newborn baby, but instead of disappointment, he agreed that we should extend our age range. We barely ate dinner that night, picking at our plates. We both felt unsure of what this meant for us and what we would even have to do to be prepared to open our home to older children, having already established a nursery. We worked tirelessly for the next month gathering items needed for two additional rooms to be included on our inspection, creating three empty bedrooms prepared for the possibility of older children, and we officially extended our age to include newborns up to age twelve. I was restless as we waited to finalize everything to receive our license. But every time I passed by the rooms, I became hopeful at the possibility of fulfilling my dream of becoming a mother. The mere thought of finally reaching this huge milestone filled my heart with gladness, and I was overjoyed.

The process had been delayed slightly, causing a new level of frustration and worry, but six months after we first started the process, we finally received our license. We were eager to fill our house with children, but time kept passing us by with no new news. Finally, three months after we received our license, we received the call from Children Services, and we both rushed home anxiously awaiting a set of siblings to arrive. We nervously checked over everything in the rooms we had prepared as we waited.

Two hours past their estimated arrival time we received a call with the news that they would not be coming to live with us after all because they were placed in kinship care with someone who stepped forward and personally knew the children. During training, we had learned this may be a possibility; however, it was our first real look at how heartbreaking foster care could be. Yet, despite that glimpse of disappointment, we were still eager to fill our home with children who needed us and so we patiently waited again.

A week later, as I was in a work meeting, Children Services called and spoke with Mike about a need for siblings to be placed in our home. During training, Mike and I had made an agreement that if one of us got a call and couldn't reach the other, we would use our best judgment after reviewing the case to decide so that we wouldn't miss out on the opportunity. When I got back to my office, I saw a text to call him. He was excited to tell me that placement would finally happen for us and to leave so we could welcome two children into our home.

I stood in the front room staring out of the window and watched as the case worker helped the children gather their belongings and ushered them towards the door. When I first saw them both, I took a deep breath to help fight the tears that were beginning to flood my eyes and nodded to Mike to open the door and welcome the children and case worker in. This was the moment we worked so hard for. In this moment, my feelings about what I once wanted more than anything no longer mattered. Those two scared faces looking up at me with uncertainty were now my priority, and I would do anything to protect them both.

To be respectful of their lives and maintain their confidentiality, I must keep the details surrounding their identities to a minimum. What I can tell you is over the next two years, I fell in love with these incredible children and considered them to be part of our family. As such, we were willing to go to great lengths to prioritize family. Mike and I agreed that I would step down from my career to focus on our children and their needs full-time. We poured so much of ourselves into setting healthy boundaries and helping them regain a sense of stability in a world filled with uncertainty. We wanted them both to know we were there for them and cared for them greatly. I was hopefully optimistic. Memories of playing with my dollhouse resurfaced as I began living my dream, painting pictures with my children as their laughter filled our home. It felt as though this was God's plan of redemption for my life and all roads led me to that exact moment in time.

Just as I was beginning to get used to this new feeling of hopeful optimism, our journey took a devastating turn. Adoption, once seemingly within our grasp, was abruptly snatched away by a whirlwind of disappointments beyond our control. I felt like I had been picked up and catapulted so hard straight into the deep end of the ocean without a life vest. Where I was once filled with hope, I now found myself thrashing my arms about for dear life desperately trying to tread water. I felt so angry—a new emotion that I had not fully experienced until this moment. I felt like I failed miserably as a mom while letting everyone down—God, my children, Mike, and, the harshest judge of all, myself. The weight of the guilt clung tightly to my ankle like an anchor, threatening to pull me under. Before I could grasp the reality of the situation, my children were gone, taken from us in a hurry. The agony on their faces will forever be etched in my memory. The pain that followed ran deep, cutting through the very core of my being.

Turning my Back on God

I felt physically ill every time I tried to look at myself in the mirror. The cruelty was unbearable. To have worked so hard for something we wanted so badly, only to have it taken from us so quickly was just unfair. I found myself withdrawing from church, unable to confront God, whom I blamed for the chaos engulfing my life. Instead of running to God, I pushed Him to the back of my mind as I tried to rebuild a life that was sustainable for me amidst the ruins of my shattered heart.

I threw myself back to work full-time and found myself in a job that challenged my creativity and opened me up in areas that, at the time, I had felt were lost. I found contentment with the overtime hours, as it kept me busy, and I didn't have to think about what I had just been through. It took two full years after losing our children before I was finally starting to experience a sense of joy again. It was then I found I could let God in a little more. I even began making plans to open a business, and not just any business but my dream business—a stationery and greeting card brand, thoughtfully designed to help lift up friends going through hardships.

Just as I was nurturing the seeds of my new ambition—laying the foundation for my new business—life had another twist in store for me. One cold March day, I was to drive back to my hometown over an hour away from where I lived to meet with two of my best friends for Sunday brunch. As I got ready, I noticed I wasn't quite feeling well. Something felt off, but I brushed it aside and grabbed a soda to help calm my stomach for the long drive. The day started out happy and fun with friends and quickly changed, yet again, to a day filled with confusion, uncertainty, pain, and sorrow. In my heart, I knew instantly what had happened—I had a miscarriage. Despite my disbelief, I kept it to myself the rest of the day until I could be certain.

The next day, after speaking with a friend at work, it became apparent that I had indeed experienced a miscarriage. What was perplexing to me was that I didn't even know I had been pregnant. I stood frozen as I stared at her, before systematically excusing myself to turn and walk back to my desk on pure adrenaline. I called my doctor's office and explained the situation. They made an appointment for me to come immediately, which I did—alone. I was still in disbelief that this could have even been a possibility, so I didn't think it would be necessary for Mike to join me at the office and to alarm him until I knew for certain there was reason to be alarmed. I texted him to let him know I was going to see my doctor to deal with what I suspected was a typical issue resurfacing with my history of having polycystic ovarian syndrome. As I drove to the doctor's office, my emotions were a whirlwind of confusion and disbelief as I talked myself into believing this was impossible.

Once I was in the exam room and alone with my thoughts, I wrestled with the decision to call Mike, ultimately choosing to shoulder the burden solo—a decision that in hindsight, I deeply regret. When my suspicions had been confirmed, I became numb and emotionless. My doctor, without any compassion whatsoever, explained to me that I would never be able to carry a child to full term. She went so far as to suggest that I stop trying to conceive altogether and find something else to focus my energy on.

In just a few heartbeats, I was tossed into a whirlwind of emotions—joy at the shock of conceiving after being told it was impossible, despair at the realization that I had lost our baby because my body couldn't sustain the pregnancy, and the crushing directive that I must come to terms with never trying for another child. A loud ringing filled my ears, and as my surroundings blurred into darkness, I closed my eyes, desperately wishing to be anywhere but there, holding back tears with all the strength I had left.

Each piece of information seemed to add weight to the anchor tethered to my ankle. First of losing our foster placement, and now of the prospect of ever having children of my own. Each blow pulling me deeper and deeper to the bottom of the ocean, landing with a giant thud as my arms and legs swung out from under me. I allowed my heart to grow cold to protect myself from any further heartache and systematically closed it off completely. The pressure of my own personal abyss was so intense that I felt silenced. Once again, I found myself unable to cry out to God because the darkness had already consumed me. It seemed as though the enemy had already won, and he had stolen from me the only thing I had ever really wanted: *Motherhood.*

The Prodigal Daughter Returns

The time I spent adrift in the murky water blurred into oblivion. I settled into a routine and lived life on autopilot for a long time—almost two years had passed so quickly. But after a while, when I finally began opening my eyes—truly seeing the underwater world around me—I noticed a light piercing the darkness from above. I squinted as I tried to make out the object just within reach. Stretching out my hand, I was desperate to grab hold of it. Yet the more I tried to reach this ray of hope shining from above, the tighter the anchor's chain seemed to tighten its grip on me. In that moment I realized there was a way out of this. All I needed to do was cry out to God, lay it all on the ocean bed, take Jesus's extended hand, and allow myself to be pulled to shore.

I lay in bed sobbing loud cries of agony over the losses I had experienced, begging God for forgiveness for turning my back on Him. I was desperate for a way out of this feeling, so I recommitted my life to God. Life had been passing by so rapidly, and I knew if I wasn't careful, it could slip away from me altogether before I even realized it.

As I drifted to sleep that night, I had a dream of being plucked from the waters and placed on the shore. My legs were wobbly beneath me as I tried to remember how to walk, I never saw who had saved me, but I knew in my heart it could only have been God.

When I woke up, I had a sense of peace that I hadn't felt in a very long time. Looking back to those heartbreaking moments, I can see now where God's grace was with me even when I was struggling in the deep waters. He never left me there alone, despite my turning away from Him. He waited patiently and lovingly for me to return to Him, on my own accord.

You are Authentically Anchored

Even after I had turned my heart back over to God, I still struggled to find purpose in my pain. The idea of ever sharing my story with anyone seemed beyond me. Until one day a moment presented itself: a stark reminder that I was firmly and authentically anchored in Christ and that He created me to do good for others. By helping others through their bottom-of-the-ocean moments to discover their authentic identity in God, the purpose of my pain crystallized before me.

There is Purpose in Your Pain

My friend, if you find yourself sitting on the ocean floor wondering if you'll ever make it to shore, I want to remind you that you were uniquely and authentically created by God in His image to be you—uniquely and individually, not to be like anyone else. The choice of who lifts your anchor is yours. Will you give in and let the enemy win, or will you hand over the chains to God, allowing Him to lovingly place you back on solid ground, firmly anchored in Him?

What you are experiencing right now is unique to your situation. While no one will ever know the magnitude of how it makes you feel, God can put people in your life who can empathize because they have walked a similar path. Finding purpose after heartache can seem impossible. Life may seem heavy for you now while anchored to the ocean depths. The very thought that your current pain could be used for a greater purpose might seem far-fetched. I understand these feelings all too well because I've been there myself and would have said the same thing. I'm not asking you to go all in on a life transformation right now. I am asking that you look up and see the hand of a loving God reaching out to you now. Grasp His extended hand and trust that things can be different as we walk this path with God and discover your identity together. I am in this with you every step of the way.

The Moment in the Mirror

Returning to the moment in the mirror, I stood there convinced that neglecting my own well-being was easier than confronting and mending my own heartache. But as I dared to confront my reflection again, I found that I didn't have pity on myself; I had sorrow. Sorrow mixed in with a lifetime of joy lovingly provided for me by God. It was in this moment of reflection that I handed over my anchor to God once and for all. I was choosing to surrender my struggles, allowing Him the chance to firmly anchor me on solid ground. This decision infused me with hope as I began to rebuild my authentic identity in Him, and suddenly, life had a whole new meaning.

This makes me wonder: How often do we turn our backs on God and on ourselves as well?

Identity Struggle

My identity was lost when I lost the only thing that I had wanted in life—to be a mother. This caused me to turn my back on God as I settled into the ocean floor.

What is something that you have faced that has caused you to feel as if your identity in christ was lost or changed?

Glimpses of Grace

Turning my back on God was something that happened during a moment when I was at my lowest. Because of the compounded series of events, I was already teetering on the edge of despair when that final blow came. That critical moment was the catalyst to give a stronghold to the enemy in my life, yet it was I who chose to walk away from God.

I had given in to the lie that I could never return to God after distancing myself from Him the way I had done, and as a result, I lingered at the bottom of the ocean longer than I should have. My friend, you don't have to stay in this state. How I wish someone would have reminded me of this truth sooner. The path back to the Father is always open; He is waiting for you with open arms. How do I know this to be true? Because His word tells us in The Parable of the Lost Son. Let's look at this together:

> *Jesus continued: "There was a man who had two sons. The younger one said to his father, 'Father, give me my share of the estate.' So he divided his property between them. Not long after that, the younger son got together all he had, set off for a distant country and there squandered his wealth in wild living. After he had spent everything, there was a severe famine in that whole country, and he began to be in need. So he went and hired himself out to a citizen of that country, who sent him to his fields to feed pigs. He longed to fill his stomach with the pods that the pigs were eating, but no one gave him anything. When he came to his senses, he said, 'How many of my father's hired servants have food to spare, and here I am starving to death! I will set out and go back to my father and say to him: Father, I have sinned against heaven and against you. I am no longer worthy to be called your son; make me like one of your hired servants.' So he got up and went to his father. But while he was still a long way off, his father saw him and was filled with compassion for him; he ran to his son, threw his arms around him and kissed him.* —Luke 15:11–20

Grace is found in the father's response to his son. Instead of scolding or rejecting him, the father sees him and runs to embrace him with affection regardless of his mistakes. Much like this father, our Father embraces us despite our mistakes; He celebrates our return and welcomes us with open arms. I was worried that by turning my back on God, He would be angry with me, but what I found instead was an overwhelming sense of peace as He welcomed me back with open arms.

The son said to him, 'Father, I have sinned against heaven and against you. I am no longer worthy to be called your son. But the father said to his servants, 'Quick! Bring the best robe and put it on him. Put a ring on his finger and sandals on his feet. Bring the fattened calf and kill it. Let's have a feast and celebrate. For this son of mine was dead and is alive again; he was lost and is found.' So they began to celebrate. —Luke 15:21–24

Grace is found in the restoration of the relationship between a father and his son. His father presents him with all these items to celebrate the return and restoration of his family. Much like this father, our Father forgives us and rejoices over the return of our lost soul when we come back to Him. The moment I prayed for forgiveness felt like the weight of the anchor had lessened as Jesus picked it up and carried it for me.

Meanwhile, the older son was in the field. When he came near the house, he heard music and dancing. So he called one of the servants and asked him what was going on. 'Your brother has come,' he replied, 'and your father has killed the fattened calf because he has him back safe and sound.' The older brother became angry and refused to go in. So his father went out and pleaded with him. But he answered his father, 'Look! All these years I've been slaving for you and never disobeyed your orders. Yet you never gave me even a young goat so I could celebrate with my friends. But when this son of yours who has squandered your property with prostitutes comes home, you kill the fattened calf for him!' 'My son,' the father said, 'you are always with me, and everything I have is yours. But we had to celebrate and be glad, because this brother of yours was dead and is alive again; he was lost and is found.' —Luke 15:25–32

Grace is found by the father pleading with his jealous son and offering him the chance to celebrate the return of his brother. Much like his father, our Father longs to be reunited with us—his children who have turned away from Him. Even though I was the one who turned my back on God, I have felt the gentle nudge to return to God more consistently as I work to rebuild our relationship.

The Heart of the Matter: Discovering Unsinkable Grace

Let's talk about what this means for us in those moments we feel we're at the bottom of the ocean. When we are sitting in the depths of despair, it is natural to feel lost, scared, and discouraged, like we are drowning, broken, and utterly alone. Doubts may cloud your mind, and questions about faith might surface, leaving you wondering about the next step.

While I don't have the answers to your unique situation, what I do have is clarity in Christ. Pulling yourself from these depths might seem impossible alone, but remember, you're not surfacing alone—Jesus is with you, empowering you with every reach. Return to your Father, cry out to Him, and place your fears and doubts on the ocean floor. Forgiveness is yours if you simply ask for it.

I can almost hear you saying, "But Shonda, I turned my back on God, surely there's no way He will forgive me." This is the same thing I said many times. My friend, the enemy wants you to believe that lie, hoping you remain captive in the darkness because he fears the light inside of you. He knows all it takes is a single spark to reignite your spirit, and he will do anything to stop that from happening. Don't let him keep you there any longer.

The greatest gift you can give yourself is that of grace—just as our Father gives us grace so we must also extend that same offering to ourselves. We put so much pressure on our shoulders that we often forget we are human just like everyone else. Next time you pass by a mirror, don't be afraid to look at the reflection staring back at you; she needs your grace. I will share another way you can challenge yourself to become more comfortable with looking at your reflection in the mirror in the next chapter.

Finding Joy

You are cherished by a loving Father. No matter how fiercely life's waves are crashing down all around you, God's grace remains unsinkable. Even during trials, have hope, and trust that the current hardship is temporary, grace will lead you to brighter shores where renewal and restoration await. You are authentically created by God in His image, perfectly crafted to be exactly who you are. It is all too common to experience a loss of identity during such trying times. Instead of focusing so much on who you aspire to be, I encourage you to embrace who you are in this very moment. Joy is found the moment you let go and allow Jesus to carry your anchor so you can get to shore.

Anchor Points

Rediscovering your authentic self and rebuilding your faith takes time. Be patient with yourself and trust that God will guide you through these exercises. Think of the following exercises as anchor points—tools designed to help you remain authentically anchored in Christ.

Before diving into these activities, make sure you have your growth bag and a journal or the companion workbook handy, as mentioned in the introduction of this book. If you haven't had a chance to read the introduction yet, now is a good time to pause and read it. Once you're up to speed, come back to this section ready to engage with the activities.

Affirm

Write the following scripture and post it somewhere you'll see it every day, maybe it's a bathroom mirror, refrigerator, or your home office. Memorize it and refer to it when you feel alone at the bottom of the ocean.

"When you pass through the waters, I will be with you; and when you pass through the rivers, they will not sweep over you. When you walk through the fire, you will not be burned; the flames will not set you ablaze." —Isaiah 43:2

Prayer

Heavenly Father, in this moment—whether I find myself sitting at the bottom of the ocean or standing on the shore—let me feel your presence now. Father, help me know that I am never alone in my struggles, that I am cherished, worthy, and enough. Please make your grace known to me in this season of my life. Give me strength to face each new day as I work on rebuilding my identity in you. Lord, thank you for extending your hand and helping me become anchored in you, Amen.

Journal Prompts

How do I feel about where I am now? Spiritually, physically, and emotionally.

_____

_____

_____

_____

_____

_____

_____

Where do I hope to be by the end of this book?

_____

_____

_____

_____

_____

_____

_____

_____

_____

_____

_____

_____

_____

_____

_____

_____

_____

_____

_____

_____

_____

_____

_____

_____

_____

_____

Declaration Statements

"I am" statement: Write a statement about who you feel you are in this very moment. *Example: I am hopeful.*

I am

_____

_____

"I hope to be" statement: Write a statement about who you hope to be by the end of this book. *Example: I hope to be confident in my identity.*

I hope to be

_____

_____

Chapter Two
Who Am I?

Coming to the surface after spending so long at the bottom of the ocean felt surreal. I had this overwhelming sense of loss—loss of time, love, hope, and identity. Adrift in the vast ocean, without a boat in sight, I felt as though I was still treading water and wondered how I would ever reach the shore.

In that moment of resurfacing, I recognized the need for action but wasn't quite sure what that action needed to be. Up until that point, my life had been shaped by others' expectations and labels, resulting in feeling like I was living a lie.

It wasn't always this way. I can remember a time when I was filled with a joy so powerful that others would ask me why I was so happy all the time. This was back when I was in high school and beginning to serve in youth ministry. That period in life feels like a lifetime ago; yet even today as I remember my time spent serving in youth ministry, I am reminded of all the lives that God brought into mine, some of whom I'm still close with today. Back then, time felt simpler, perhaps a reflection of my youthful naivety.

It started when I was attending one of the most incredible places I have ever had the privilege of being a part of: *The Barn*. The Barn was a haven for me. It was a place where I could dare to be myself, no matter how awkward or weird I thought I was. Sure, it wasn't free from the bullying I would receive within the walls of the school, as some of it did follow me into this environment, but regardless, the experiences I had within those walls were truly life changing.

After graduation, I continued to help as much as I could and served alongside some amazing individuals. One of my favorite memories during this time was when I chaperoned a music festival where we camped out in tents. The girls, packed in the tent like sardines, keeping me up all night with their endless giggling. As I struggled to get them to go to sleep, I ended up giving in and joining the fun. It makes me chuckle thinking back to their convincing me to let them braid my hair with the one caveat that it had to be upside down. The next day I even allowed them to convince me to let them spray my hair with blue and green colors, one on each side. I may have looked odd, but those memories are still with me today and those girls made a lasting impact on my heart.

I also spent many late evenings inside the walls of that old barn praying with others; listening to their struggles, concerns, hopes, and dreams; and celebrating with them when they had achieved the impossible. I would often get there before anyone else to help Larry, the owner, open The Barn before the drove of kids flocked in. As I went through my duties, I daydreamed about the possibility of one day opening my own haven of sorts to be a place where people would come to gather and make new friends. At the time, it felt impossible, so I pushed that seed to the back of my mind hoping to one day revisit.

My mentor and friend, Larry, is someone who I will be forever grateful for. While Larry has since gone on to be with the Lord, he is one of the first people I will search for when I reach Heaven's gate. He encouraged me to follow God's guidance in my life, his favorite saying was, *"planting seeds, trusting God."* I wish he were still here today to see the seed he planted years ago is still making a difference in my life today.

As time went on and life began to take shape, I found myself getting married and moving away from the area where I had served for so many years in ministry. It was only a short time before I moved back after my divorce. The only difference in my return was me; I was different. I had moved back after my divorce to be near family and friends as I healed from disappointment and looked for meaning in my new and unexpected phase of life. My divorce wasn't what caused me to find myself at the bottom of the ocean, but it did contribute to the weight of the anchor chain. It took a long time for me to find my footing again, a few years to be exact, and while I try to live my life with no regrets, I do regret allowing temptation to consume and mold me into a version of myself I am not proud of.

I was twenty-five and suddenly didn't know who I was anymore, but I was desperate to figure that out. I heard my friends when they told me

I hadn't truly lived life or tried new things because I had been so rigid and disciplined up until this point. So, I quickly found myself joining in. I became more and more reckless as I hosted gatherings every weekend that always ended with me regretting my choice to chase lemonade after tequila. This was the first time I can remember taking my eyes off Jesus. While I know I was a woman in need of direction during those years, I am thankful for the friendships I established during that time. God used those friendships to help me get back on track.

Spark of Life Dimmed Instantly

Recently, I was having a really hard day where no matter what I did or said, it was the wrong thing. Discouraged, I walked out of my office and into the bathroom to face myself in the mirror. Ever since my rise from the bottom of the ocean, this was something I challenged myself to do every time I struggle with believing in my capabilities to remind myself that I am only human—I will make mistakes, I will struggle, I will get it wrong sometimes and that's okay.

As I struggled to remember who I was now that I have resurfaced, I remembered who I used to be back in my younger years during my time serving in youth ministry: joyful. I was most joyful when I was serving in a capacity that God guided me to do. I desperately longed to return to that state of unending joy, shining my own light so that others could find their way back to God in the darkness. But I wondered: *How do I get there?* While I was aware of how far I had come from my time anchored to the bottom of the ocean without a lifeline, I longed to feel the joy deep inside that I once had. I hungered for more.

My mind was blank, nothing was coming to me as I stared at my reflection, except these three words: *Who am I?* At first, I asked the question quietly in my head, but after being met with a frustrating silence, I asked aloud, with a shout, *"Who am I?!"* Startled at the sound of my own voice, I chuckled as I locked eyes with myself in the mirror and answered my question with brutal honesty: *"You're so weird, people would think you're crazy if they saw you."*

As silly as this moment seemed to be, what it uncovered was a new spark of life. I could see it in my own reflection as I jolted myself from the harsh sound of my own voice bouncing off the mirror and then again when I chuckled. It was there, with my hands on my hips, that I surrendered my life in a whole new way. It was reassuring, giving me the contentment in believing it was okay for me not to know who I was just yet. I realized that discovering my authentic self was still unfolding, and would continue to unfold, before my very eyes.

Contentment was something that rarely happened to me; as a result, I recognized this as growth within me and went back to my desk to work. Sitting at my desk, I couldn't help but wonder what that spark of life I saw was all about. However, with a deadline approaching, I decided to bottle this thought to explore later when time permitted.

This experience highlighted a coping mechanism I've developed over time: busyness. Pouring myself into work and creating never-ending to-do lists allows me to redirect my mind to something other than the problem at hand. This toxic trait of mine would often be at my own detriment, as I could only run on fumes for so long before I would crash and burn and be forced into rest only to repeat the process all over.

However, between work and the persistent nagging question of identity throughout the day, my stress grew more and more intense. I had been met with a moment of criticism that caused doubt in myself and in my skills. I know that I am a graphic designer who has experience across a wider range than others, but not everyone has seen me put this into action. This got me thinking. When others don't believe in our capabilities or give us the chance to show our talents, it is frustrating. Instead of confidently proving my abilities to my critic, I silently picked up the label handed to me that read *unqualified*. I allowed this label to define me, changing my perceived work identity from Graphic Designer to Unqualified Graphic Designer.

The Weight of Labels

As my workday drew to a close, I knew I couldn't move on to anything else until I explored these feelings more. It was like one of those annoying moments where something bugs you so much you want to stop everything you are doing to get this one thing done, and you know you can't rest until you do.

I grabbed a sheet of paper and wrote the word 'unqualified' on it. I let my mind focus on all the labels I had ever picked up from others and wrote them down on the page. Reading over them, I realized there were some labels I had put on myself that I hadn't written in, so I added those to the list that had already become so long there wasn't any more room on the page.

I pictured myself back in the ocean, each of these labels the weights added to the anchor chained around my leg and threatening to pull me back down again. But how do I rid myself of these labels?

Romans chapter 8 lovingly reminds us of the only label we need to pick up:

The Spirit himself testifies with our spirit that we are God's children. Now if we are children, then we are heirs—heirs of God and co-heirs with Christ, if indeed we share in his sufferings in order that we may also share in his glory.—Romans 8:16–17

Reading through the labels I had picked up saddened me. I realized when joy was removed from my life I became unauthentic and unrecognizable. It made perfect sense that I didn't know who I was because I allowed so many others to tell me instead of trusting who God says I am—His child!

This harsh reality broke me that day. I went to bed that night troubled. Unable to sleep, I lay there as I stared at the ceiling and asked God, *"Who am I, Lord?"* I was met with silence other than the unanswered question echoing back at me in the whirl of the fan. I decided perhaps I asked the question incorrectly, so I tried again. *"Lord, please show me who I am."* Exhaustion overtook me, and I fell asleep mid-prayer, something that happened regularly as a result of working long hours.

The next day, as I walked by the mirror, I stopped and looked at my reflection. *"WHO AM I?!"* I shouted at myself. What followed surprised me. I laughed hysterically at myself, unable to stop as tears streamed down my face. I recognized the silliness of this exercise I had challenged myself to do because I knew better than anyone else that my story wasn't finished being written yet and that was okay.

You Are God's Child

I had concluded that to answer my own question, I needed to remember where I was in this current season of life. I was no longer on the bottom of the ocean, but I also wasn't yet standing on the shore. While Jesus may have reached His hand out to help me to the surface, I was keeping myself there, treading water as I held my anchor. I had been determined to figure this out on my own.

As I scrolled through social media and compared myself to the happy faces on my screen, it caused me to sink a little more and more. Every label I picked back up and put on myself weighed me down, and soon, I struggled to keep my head above water again.

How easy it was for me to give up after having fought my way off of that ocean floor surprised me. Perhaps I hadn't fully trusted that God would bring me through this. I turned my phone off, stood up, and marched myself to the mirror.

"*Who am I?*" I asked, in a calmer, more loving voice. "*I am a child of God.*" I smiled at the woman staring back at me, and with confidence, I said, "*Yes, yes you are, and you are so very loved as you are.*"

This reassurance was all I needed to shift my mindset. By trying to fit into someone else's mold of who I should be and never allowing myself the chance to be my authentic self, I changed the course of my own life. I can easily pinpoint pockets of time that contributed to my lack of self-esteem. As a child being made fun of for the gap in my teeth or the clothing I wore; as a teenager who wasn't part of the 'in crowd', being left out of gatherings and being ignored at the ones I did get invited to, or worse yet being the punchline in every joke; as a young adult facing a heartbreak so big I didn't know if I would ever find love again; and as an adult being told that no one will listen to me because of how I look.

If I pulled off all the labels I had picked up and put on myself, they would be stacked so high they would fall over, but I knew I had to let them go. I picked up my paper with labels and read them again. As my tears fell onto the paper, the ink began to run. I prayed, giving it all over to God; asking Him to free me from the labels others had put on me. I sought out forgiveness for holding on to these labels for as long as I had, and I also offered up forgiveness for those who had put them on me. After my prayer, my first thought was to rip it up into tiny pieces and throw it away, so I did.

Who Do You Want to Be?

Friend, it is so easy to be influenced by the thoughts and opinions of others. When we allow the noise to enter our minds, we are giving them free reign over us to take up precious and valuable space, and in doing this, we are shutting out God. The less space we allow for God to speak to us, the less we will hear Him.

I found that eventually I stopped talking to others first about my situation and started talking more about it to God. Having a personal encounter with Jesus became my mission because one thing I remembered was James 4:8, *"Come near to God, and he will come near to you."*

The best way to begin having a personal encounter with Jesus is to start doing daily devotions. I knew that one thing I had to replace was time spent on social media, so I downloaded an app that offers free devotions, and with the support of a very dear friend—*you know who you are*—she and I banded together in daily devotions which we still carry out today.

In addition to the daily devotions, try to make a conscious effort to commit to prayer at a time that you won't fall asleep in the middle of talking with God. Showing up for God fully to give Him the space to work is important and shows Him you are committed to seeking His direction.

Every new label picked up thereafter that weighs you down and threatens to sink you again, go to God in prayer, laying it at His feet.

Over time, the removal of the labels and deeper connection with Jesus helped me to shore. As I stood on solid ground once more, I realized that I made it here safely because Jesus carried my anchor for me to help lighten my load. It was His way of showing me that I can be authentically anchored in Him as I begin to uncover what life has in store for me as ordained by God. I want to confidently be authentically me.

This brings up a new question: Who do you want to be?

Identity Struggle

When I relied solely on the opinions of others, I lost sight of who I was created to be. I allowed myself to be weighed down by the number of labels put on me by others, causing me to be pulled below water again. I would get so wrapped in wanting to belong to a group of individuals that was fun to be around, encouraged me, and helped lift my spirits when I was down. I longed for that feeling of community I had during my time spent at The Barn.

When we face hardships, we may find ourselves in a more negative mindset than usual. It happens without us realizing it most of the time until one day, you're scrolling social media, and a quick judgmental thought enters your mind about the person you are looking at. We mean well, but often, the reality of our own dire situation blinds us from seeing the good around us with what He has already given us. It's a natural survival instinct to want to be someone that others accept, even if that means not being who we are authentically.

By choosing to live our lives in a way that puts a false version of ourselves, we are giving others the chance to control our lives in a way that pushes God outside as they preoccupy His seat. It's ok to be you, flaws and all, imperfectly perfect in Christ.

How many times do we push God outside of our lives to give His seat to others?

Glimpses of Grace

It's easy to want to be someone else, to live a life that isn't our own, when ours doesn't look promising. Comparison often leads to us picking up new labels that we may not really need to add to our ever-growing stack. When we feel left out because of who we are or because of our past, it's hard to find grace in the moments we are shunned by others.

The story of The Woman at the Well is a good reminder that to be fully free to be ourselves, we should dare be bold enough to converse with Jesus. By opening up to God about your situation, you are giving Him the space to offer you a refreshing drink from the living water. Let's take a look at her story:

> When a Samaritan woman came to draw water, Jesus said to her, 'Will you give me a drink?' (His disciples had gone into the town to buy food.) The Samaritan woman said to him, 'You are a Jew, and I am a Samaritan woman. How can you ask me for a drink?' (For Jews do not associate with Samaritans.) Jesus answered her, 'If you knew the gift of God and who it is that asks you for a drink, you would have asked him, and he would have given you living water.' 'Sir,' the woman said, 'you have nothing to draw with, and the well is deep. Where can you get this living water? Are you greater than our father Jacob, who gave us the well and drank from it himself, as did also his sons and his livestock?' Jesus answered, 'Everyone who drinks this water will be thirsty again, but whoever drinks the water I give them will never thirst. Indeed, the water I give them will become in them a spring of water welling up to eternal life.' The woman said to him, 'Sir, give me this water so that I won't get thirsty and have to keep coming here to draw water.'—John 4:7–15

Grace is found when Jesus speaks to the Samaritan woman. Culturally, they should not have been associated with one another, but Jesus spoke to her regardless. Similarly, Jesus wants to be associated with you, as you are. Grace is also found in the living water—Jesus offers the Samaritan woman a new life and salvation. Have you ever been so thirsty you drink a full bottle of water and still can't quench your thirst? Could you imagine a life where you wouldn't ever get thirsty again and need water? When I was desperate to get to the shore, I was parched, longing to have my spiritual thirst quenched and be transformed in Christ once more.

He told her, 'Go, call your husband and come back.' 'I have no husband,' she replied. Jesus said to her, 'You are right when you say you have no husband. The fact is, you have had five husbands, and the man you now have is not your husband. What you have just said is quite true.'—John 4:16–18

Grace is found when Jesus accepts the Samaritan woman despite knowing her past. He doesn't fault her or shame her for what she's done, even though she may have faced judgment because Jesus, a Jewish man, engaged her in a conversation. This part of the story gives me hope for a future where we don't judge others based on their past mistakes, yet we still love one another and lift each other up in prayer and encouragement. While others may not have extended grace to you in your depth of despair, you can still extend grace to others in theirs.

'Sir,' the woman said, 'I can see that you are a prophet. Our ancestors worshiped on this mountain, but you Jews claim that the place where we must worship is in Jerusalem.' 'Woman,' Jesus replied, 'believe me, a time is coming when you will worship the Father neither on this mountain nor in Jerusalem. You Samaritans worship what you do not know; we worship what we do know, for salvation is from the Jews. Yet a time is coming and has now come when the true worshipers will worship the Father in the Spirit and in truth, for they are the kind of worshipers the Father seeks. God is spirit, and his worshipers must worship in the Spirit and in truth.' The woman said, 'I know that Messiah' (called Christ) 'is coming. When he comes, he will explain everything to us.' Then Jesus declared, 'I, the one speaking to you—I am he.'—John 4:19–26

Grace is found when Jesus teaches the Samaritan woman about what it means to worship in spirit and in truth. He explains to her the importance of faith in this moment, in a way that shows us that He is gently guiding her to a relationship with the Father. He longs for you to worship God in spirit and in truth. Grace is also found when Jesus reveals Himself as the Messiah; He reveals his authentic identity. Revealing who we are authentically is a moment of truth, acceptance of ourselves, and in a way, acceptance of others we trust to see the real us in our moments of weakness. If I had it to do all over again, I would have shown my critic how capable I am by extending grace in the moment and working together towards a better resolution.

The Heart of the Matter: Let Go of Labels

Let's talk about what this means in our 'who am I' moment. Our past is something we cannot change; it follows us wherever we go. What we can change, however, is how we allow it to define who we are today.

Friend, give yourself some grace, you have likely been treading water for far too long. When we put expectations on ourselves that are impossible to meet, we are only setting ourselves up for future disappointment. Shed those labels, one by one remove them, and throw them away.

I am giving you permission to start fresh, with no expectations, no requirements, and no labels. Who are you without the labels? What does it feel like for you to remove them? For me, it was like a deep exhale after holding my breath for what felt like years followed by sheer panic as I stood frozen wondering what was next.

It's completely natural to not know what to do once you've removed all the noise, which is why I want to remind you that this is the moment you invite Jesus in. Let Him take up space in your life, let Him show you where and how you can drink from the living water, and let Him guide you to the life that is meant for you to live. Only when we remove everything, stripping it way back to the most vulnerable state possible, is when we can allow Jesus to take up full residence. Jesus wants to reconcile with you. Will you allow Him the chance?

Finding Joy Again

My friend, in our brokenness, God cares for us and calls us His own. It's ok if you feel alone and uncertain about who you are and where you are headed. You can give it all to God and trust that He will pull you out and place you on solid ground once more. On days when you feel alone in your struggles, go to God; pull up a seat next to you, and invite Him to join you. In the next chapter, I share with you how entering a season of solitude helps us draw nearer to God more frequently. Joy is found on the other side of letting go, in the sweet surrender to His plan and timing.

Anchor Points

Rediscovering your authentic self and rebuilding your faith takes time. Be patient with yourself and trust that God will guide you through these exercises. Each exercise is meant to be an anchor point keeping you authentically anchored in Christ.

Affirm

Write the following scripture somewhere you will see it daily. Memorize it, and refer to it when you lose faith in who you are.

"See what great love the Father has lavished on us, that we should be called children of God! And that is what we are! The reason the world does not know us is that it did not know him." —1 John 3:1

Prayer

Heavenly Father, so many labels have been put on my shoulders that I no longer want to continue carrying. I pray that you give me strength and courage to remove every single label that doesn't serve me anymore. Help me to only pick up the one that matters most in this moment. I am your child, God. I pray that as the labels fall off, you help me reach the shore and find my footing on solid ground once more. I pray that you continue to work in me as I complete this book, opening myself up to allow more space for you in my life. Thank you, Lord, for carrying my anchor, Amen.

Exercise and Journal Prompt

Exercise: What labels have I picked up and placed on myself? Write down every single one on a sheet of paper, pray over it, rip it up, and toss it.

Journal Prompt: Write about what you experienced during the exercise, what you let go of, and how it made you feel.

_____

_____

_____

_____

_____

_____

_____

_____

_____

_____

_____

_____

_____

Declaration Statements

"I am" statement: Write a statement about who you feel you are in this very moment. *Example: I am free to be me.*

I am

_____

_____

"I hope to be" statement: Write a statement about who you hope to be by the end of this book. *Example: I hope to be able to shed the weight of the labels.*

I hope to be

_____

_____

Chapter Three
Never Truly Alone

After being in the depths of the ocean and then treading water on the surface, I now find my feet back on solid ground, but the legs beneath me feel shaky and unfamiliar as I try to find my footing. Throughout my life, the value of friendship has been a constant beacon, guiding me through both calm and turbulent waters. Friendship is something that has been and will always be important to me. It's easy to find surface level acquaintances, those who have gotten to know me on the surface. While they have inspired, encouraged, and supported me in my times of distress—something I am forever grateful for—the search for deeper bonds is daunting. Finding those rare gems who chose to get to know me on a deeper level and yet still accept me, messy and all, has always been challenging for me.

Growing up, I often found myself the center of attention, but not in any way I would have hoped. I seemed to be an easy target for others to focus on, hurling insults my way. I was often made fun of for my appearance or how I spoke, my classmates laughed and pointed at me as tears would fall down my face. I never understood, and often still question today, how others could be so mean to someone who was different than they were, especially in childhood. I carried this pain with me for a very long time—recalling the names of each classmate who hurt me, along with what they said or did. I can count on one hand the number of true friends I had in school who accepted me and embraced me for who I was.

Because of my childhood experiences, as an adult, I learned quickly that I had created a circle of friendships with many different levels to protect my heart. I got to pick who I allowed in each section of my circle of friendship, reserving the innermost level only for those I fully trusted with my vulnerabilities. I would open myself up to them in ways that not everyone got to see. I would tell them my secrets, trusting they would guard them as their own. People would come and go in my life often, moving in and out from each level, but the one constant I had was the safety net of my sacred inner circle; until one day, I didn't.

It felt like everything happened in a whirlwind. A disagreement formed between me and one of my closest friends, leaving me stunned and unsure of how to mend the divide caused. As I tried to wrap my head around what was happening, another bombshell dropped—a mutual friend forwarded me messages from a group chat where my private insecurities about my appearance and my infertility were being mocked behind my back. Confronting my friend about this betrayal only led to denial, despite the evidence I had in my hands. I was absolutely devastated by the betrayal of trust.

I completely shut down. Full stop. I felt betrayed, shamed, and ridiculed. As a result, I constructed walls around my heart so fast that it impacted every single person in my inner circle as it forced them to the next level. I didn't want to speak, see, or be near anyone. I just wanted to be left alone. I made the choice to retreat into a season of solitude. It was something I had never done before, but then again, ending a friendship with someone who was in my inner circle was nothing I had ever experienced before.

The younger version of me was a person who was filled with compassion, light, love, and forgiveness. I would forgive those who hurt me a million times over, each time a piece of my heart would be plucked away, until little by little my heart had been filled with so many holes there was nothing more to give. Having recently come to shore, I was still on shaky ground when my friendship ended, which contributed to those holes growing bigger. I became the type of person who was at the point of not caring anymore, about others and about myself; my heart grew cold and desolate. I was still in the in-between where I was working towards softening and leading with love.

The events that led up to the moment of the ended friendship still feel like a bad dream to me. Feelings were hurt—mine and hers—our friendship ended, and really that is all that matters in the *details* of this situation.

The lesson learned from this situation is one that shifted my entire being. I had never experienced the level of hurt that I felt from ending a friendship of this caliber. I questioned everything from am I a terrible friend, why don't people care how I feel, will anyone ever listen to me, do I not deserve to be a mother, why am I so unlovable, what did I do to deserve to be treated this way, and more.

No one had prepared me for the grief I would experience at what felt like the death of a friendship. My friend hadn't died, but the relationship felt as though it did. There was no time limit I could put on the length of grief I had for her; some may say I still grieve the loss of that friendship today, and they'd be right.

I knew that the only way I could find the answers to the million questions running through my mind was solitude. I needed to process, and for me, processing had to be done alone. At first, I was angry for many days, so angry that I couldn't focus on anything else. Until one day, I was sad. I cried off and on all day, wishing I could pick up the phone and call her, but I scolded myself for being weak and wanting to forgive so quickly.

Forgiving Especially When Its Hard

This brought up the realization that I hadn't fully forgiven all who had hurt me, and I knew many verses in the Bible address this, which tells us it's important. The verse that kept coming to mind was, *"Do not judge, and you will not be judged. Do not condemn, and you will not be condemned. Forgive, and you will be forgiven"* (Luke 6:37).

When it comes to judging, we all know that when we've experienced rejection or pain it's easy to judge the other person involved, even if we shouldn't. That slip of the tongue can be swift and merciless in our anger. Condemning someone goes hand in hand with judging them. We disapprove of their actions, or who they are as a person. Forgiveness is the hardest part of this lesson; Jesus tells us in order for us to be forgiven we must first forgive.

As I read this verse over and over, trying to convince myself to do the right thing like a defiant teenager, I rolled my eyes and said, *"Fine, Lord,*

I forgive her." Then, I went about my day, but I continued to wonder: *Had I really forgiven her?*

I found that simply stating a prayer of forgiveness isn't enough to get the job done, it was merely surface level on the outer ring of friendship. Forgiveness isn't something I can just say I offer; I must truly extend it from my heart, with all that I am, and then let it go to God.

Solitude Leads to Connection

The words that ended that friendship left me feeling paralyzed in place for a long time. These words played on repeat in my mind before I finally embraced solitude in the way God intended solitude to be spent, which is in prayer. On days when I felt the weight of the emotions I was struggling with, I would stop what I was doing and I would pray. On some of my worst days, I would fast for most of the day, shut off all communication with others, and fill every moment I could with prayer. I remember pleading with God for relief from the turmoil this loss was causing me.

As time went on, I continued to pray, study, and allow God into my life more and more every day. I cried out to Him, pouring out every emotion, fear, and vulnerability I had held onto for so long. I established my inner circle of only He and I, creating a space where our connection could grow stronger. Finally, something in me began to shift as I replaced these painful memories of the ended friendship with truth, scripture, and the lessons my Heavenly Father was teaching me.

It was in this quiet season of solitude with the Father where God helped me transition from being someone who had become cold and distant to someone who was warm and filled with compassion again. This shift had me questioning the power of solitude when spent with God.

I no longer clung to the pain that had shrouded that period of my life. One morning during prayer, the tears came flooding as I asked for forgiveness for the part I played in the ended friendship, for judging and condemning her actions, for shutting the door so quickly, and for not giving her a formal goodbye at the end. I ended the prayer forgiving her for everything that had happened and asked God to bless her as I let her go.

In the moments after the prayer, I found myself at my desk, pen in hand, writing her a letter. I poured my heart out on paper, I shared with her how disappointed I was and how vulnerable and insecure in the moment the situation had made me. I shared how I felt like I wasn't valued as her friend. I also owned up to my expectations and recognized that assigning blame was futile, as we had never established those boundaries to begin with. Concluding the letter, I wrote, *"I forgive you, I bless you, I release you,"* and signed my name with a sense of finality.

I held on to that letter for a short time knowing that one more act was in store that would facilitate the closure I sensed was at hand. Mike and I had a camping trip coming up and I decided to take it with me so I could put it into the fire. To me, burning the letter was more than just an act of letting go; it was a ceremonial release of the emotions entangled in that episode of my life, a symbolic gesture of moving forward from the pain that had once held me captive.

Fully Let Go

In my journey, God has shown me that people can be cruel, uttering words that may cut me to my core. Even though they may hurt me, God has a bigger plan that involves me, and I must fully let go to keep moving ahead. I have witnessed first-hand that it's during our most vulnerable times when God reminds us we are still authentically anchored to Him. He helps us to be authentically who we are in even the direst of situations. He is equipping us as we go through hardships and is nudging us to use them for good. We come out of these hard times equipped to help someone else who feels betrayed and alone, with a kindness they may never have experienced.

I believe God used this situation as a wakeup call, reminding me that pain often comes from those closest to us and not just from strangers on the internet. He used this situation to both toughen and soften me in ways that were necessary for me to be able to sit here today, watching the sun come up over the water, mesmerized by the pinks, purples, and yellows as they dance across the surface, and fully feel His presence—a reminder that I was safe on shore now. Prior to this, I was at the bottom of the ocean, desperate to get out, unsure of His presence. But now, I can feel Him all around me and all is right within.

Making the choice to enter a season of prayerful solitude was a deliberate and thoughtful decision, not to be taken lightly. If you're considering a similar path, make a plan that works with your lifestyle and be sure to set clear boundaries with those who reach out to you frequently, ensuring distractions are kept to a minimum during your time in prayer.

My friend, we do not need to fear this kind of prayerful solitude, for fear is a tool of the enemy. It is used to trip us, ensuring that when we fall; he can keep us captive at the bottom of the ocean indefinitely. If you have experienced something similar, I encourage you to have hope today and remember that God uses everything in our lives. The ending of a friendship can be used for the good according to His will if you lay it down before him as I have done. I know that it feels heavy. This feeling of solitude can be scary. Feeling like you don't have someone to sit with you and hold your hand can cause you to wonder if you'll ever get through this moment in time. But remember, you're never truly alone. God is with you even now.

I invite you to close your eyes, take in a deep breath, exhale. Do you feel that? You are not alone. As I write these words, I am picturing you and I envision myself reaching out my hand to you as a sister, offering you comfort. While in heart, I am there with you, better still, God is there with you. He has never left you; He has lovingly stood beside you holding your heavy anchor for you, just waiting on your invitation into your heart. Will you let Him in?

Whether you are about to begin a season of prayerful solitude or are already in one because you've lost your support during this trying time, I want to encourage you to see this as an opportunity to lean into this time alone with God.

Maximize Your Time in Prayerful Solitude

The amount of time you spend set aside with God and the perimeters you establish are up to you, and you alone. I will share with you what I did and what that did for me to give you an example of how you can best spend time alone with God to deepen your connection.

Let someone know: even if you cannot think of anyone you want to know that you are going to pull back a bit so you can focus inward, find one person you can let know. In the beginning, I only told Mike, because he was in the house with me, and he needed to know why I was going to be scarce from time to time. Don't feel like you owe anyone an explanation as to why you are making this choice, the choice is yours alone to make. I found that not everyone understood or even accepted my choice, and I had to be ok with that to keep moving ahead. I needed this time alone with God to heal.

Put on the full armor: you will be the most vulnerable in this state, so it is wise to put on the full armor of God. Make sure that during your moments of solitude you have a Bible close by so you can dig deep into the word. You'll also want to make sure you have the helmet of salvation at the ready, it's my favorite piece of armor as it helps to protect against the negative thoughts that will creep in during this time.

Finally, be strong in the Lord and in his mighty power. Put on the full armor of God so that you can take your stand against the devil's schemes. For our struggle is not against flesh and blood, but against the rulers, against the authorities, against the powers of this dark world and against the spiritual forces of evil in the heavenly realms. Therefore put on the full armor of God, so that when the day of evil comes, you may be able to stand your ground, and after you have done everything, to stand. Stand firm then, with the belt of truth buckled around your waist, with the breastplate of righteousness in place, and with your feet fitted with the readiness that comes from the gospel of peace. In addition to all this, take up the shield of faith, with which you can extinguish all the flaming arrows of the evil one. Take the helmet of salvation and the sword of the Spirit, which is the word of God. And pray in the Spirit on all occasions with all kinds of prayers and requests. With this in mind, be alert and always keep on praying for all the Lord's people. —Ephesians 6:10–18

Set your time: due to our schedules, it is often hard to do a full stop isolation tactic. I knew I couldn't be in solitude one hundred percent of my time, instead, I picked time slots where I could retreat to somewhere that no one else would be—usually, this was in my bedroom or another room in the house but sometimes would be in a secluded outdoor area that not many people frequent. At the very least, I recommend an hour a day, but on hard days, I have gone up to nine hours in solitude.

Remove distractions: during solitude, distractions will stop you from leaning into God fully. As you walk into your space, keep your phone outside of the space if possible. If it must come in with you in case of emergencies, at the very least, silence it or put it on do not disturb.

Get clear on your ask: it is important to know what it is you are asking God to do during this time. In the beginning, it was as simple as asking God to give me strength to get over the heartache I was feeling. Eventually, it shifted to asking God to make known the purpose my life has and what my role in His kingdom is.

What to do in solitude: the first time I was purposeful in my time spent in solitude, I remember sitting there and looking around. I reached for my phone only to realize it wasn't there and everything just felt weird. Silence can be intimidating. It is important to make sure you have all the tools you need with you; this is where my growth bag came in to save the day more than once. I would journal, study, pray, and journal some more. The most important thing to do during this time is to invite God to join you where you are, and once you do that, the rest is up to you and Him. Converse, lay it all out, be open with Him and with yourself.

In the end, during my time in solitude with the Lord, I have come to realize that I had put so much of my hope in others instead of in God. Something I have come to realize is, perhaps by putting my hope in my friendships I end up setting us all up for future failure, myself and my friends, as this ends up placing unrealistic expectations on us all. Friendship is something to be celebrated; it should be an encouraging relationship, filled with love and support. By removing the unrealistic expectations I put on others, I allow them the chance to show up in ways that surprise me and fill my life with gratitude, versus disappointment. It also challenges me to show up in encouraging, supportive ways for them regardless of my season in life.

My friend, let me encourage you to put your hope in the Lord, and the Lord alone. Ask Him to show you any areas in your own life where you have misplaced hope in others. God is your one and only constant life, He will never leave you or forsake you (Deuteronomy 31:6).

Identity Struggle

Perhaps you have found yourself in friendships that feel surface level and fracture easily, unsure of how to stop the cycle from repeating. It's important to remember that just as you hurt your friend also might be hurting. If either of you are not living life authentically, the friendship will always suffer. It's exhausting to pretend to be someone else around others, and I understand the reasoning behind wanting to do it. It's easier to be that version when others react so positively, but ask yourself: Is being someone else honoring who God created you to be?

I have come to realize that I am not for everyone, just as everyone is not for me. I know that I sometimes make clouded decisions in choosing who I keep company with. God sometimes provides an exit for those who are taking up space that is reserved for Him and those He chooses to bring into your life.

Are you harboring resentment towards someone who has hurt you instead of forgiving them as God has forgiven you? There is grace for you my friend.

Glimpses of Grace

It's a good idea to practice solitude with God to regroup and let Him help you regain a sense of direction, especially in those seasons of loneliness and self-doubt. Anna, a woman introduced to us in the Bible, stands out as one who is a great example of this in practice. Anna found solace and purpose in her dedication to God through her life of solitude as told in the second chapter of Luke. Let's look at this story together:

> *There was also a prophet, Anna, the daughter of Penuel, of the tribe of Asher. She was very old; she had lived with her husband seven years after her marriage, and then was a widow until she was eighty-four. She never left the temple but worshiped night and day, fasting and praying. Coming up to them at that very moment, she gave thanks to God and spoke about the child to all who were looking forward to the redemption of Jerusalem.* —Luke 2:36–38

Grace is found in Anna's faithfulness despite her grief. She dedicated her time to worshiping God, day and night, in the temple. Grace is also found in God, giving Anna the strength to remain steadfast in her faith. Because of the two, together, Anna goes on to speak about the child (Jesus) to others. Much like Anna, God is the only one who can give us strength during our times of rejection. By dedicating your time to worshiping Him, you are drawing nearer to uncovering layers within yourself that either have been forgotten about or discovered for the first time. I found grace in the moments of solitude I spent with God as He continued to work on softening my heart so I could let others in again.

The Heart of the Matter: Solitude for Self-Reflection

Let's talk about what this means in our moments of feeling alone or abandoned. The ending of a relationship feels heavy and can make us question our worth, it can make us angry or sad at the other person involved, or it can paralyze us in place causing us to lose all hope.

Entering a season of intentional solitude with the Lord doesn't have to be a scary thing, it should be a time of anticipation, where you draw closer to God, seeking Him for answers in your situation. It is a time of letting go of the advice and words showered on you by others. Whether you give yourself one hour a day in solitude for prayer or take a break from being socially active for a longer period of time, the choice is yours to make; only you know what you need in order to open your heart up to the possibility of trusting others again.

Our hearts, which are naturally tender, can swiftly transition from warmth and kindness to detached and cool when confronted by life's tough challenges. The best way to stop the pendulum from swinging from one end to the other so frequently is by seeking the Lord asking Him to mend what has been broken. Hardship inevitably changes us, yet through God's grace, we find a path back to a more genuine expression of ourselves, embracing the authenticity that trials have refined within us.

Finding Joy

Self-reflection, while difficult, is a vital process helping you to learn more about yourself and giving you the opportunity to be silent, hearing what God has to say. Once we allow ourselves to listen, God will begin to show us the beauty around us—I'll address this in the next chapter. Learning from the ending of a friendship is difficult, I've discovered that my time spent in solitude brings me closer to God. It's in these quiet moments I've asked Him to reveal my shortcomings in the friendship and how I might improve as a friend going forward. At the heart of this journey is the act of forgiveness. Moving forward was impossible until I had extended forgiveness not just to her but to myself as well. Joy is found in forgiveness.

Anchor Points

Rediscovering your authentic self and rebuilding your faith takes time. Be patient with yourself and trust that God will guide you through these exercises. Each exercise is meant to serve as an anchor point keeping you authentically anchored in Christ.

Affirm

Write the following scripture somewhere you will see it daily. Memorize it, and refer to it when you lose faith in who you are.

"He says, 'Be still, and know that I am God; I will be exalted among the nations, I will be exalted in the earth.'"—Psalm 46:10

Prayer

Heavenly Father, I lift up my friend who is currently reading my book. Lord, her heart is weary, she feels alone and rejected by forces beyond her control. She isn't sure what the right next steps are and she has lost her sense of identity as a result of putting her hope in others. Lord, I pray that you help her put her hope back in you. That you open her heart to love and be loved again. I pray, Lord, that you remind her that she is authentically created to be the most beautiful person ever—herself. Lord, I lift her up to you, Amen.

Journal Prompt

Reflecting on the lessons of the chapter, I encourage you to enter a time of prayerful solitude. You select the duration you need to invite God in to help you complete this prompt.

Finish this sentence: *The thought of a season of solitude makes me feel...*

_____

_____

_____

_____

_____

_____

_____

_____

_____

_____

_____

_____

_____

_____

_____

_____

_____

_____

_____

_____

_____

_____

_____

_____

_____

_____

_____

_____

_____

_____

Declaration Statements

"I am" statement: Write a statement about who you feel you are in this very moment. *Example: I am never alone.*

I am

_____

_____

"I hope to be" statement: Write a statement about who you hope to be by the end of this book. *Example: I hope to be closer to God.*

I hope to be

_____

_____

Chapter Four

Seeing the Beauty in God's Design

Sitting alone on the porch wrapped in a blanket with a hot cup of coffee, I watched the sun come up over the trees. I was praying for direction and asked God to help me feel, know, and understand my life up to this point.

The path I have traveled was rocky and curvy. It had many peaks and valleys, all of which led up to this very moment. I knew I had a choice—I could either reject life as I'd known it and continue to live in avoidance at the bottom of the ocean, or I could choose to accept my life by God's design despite it looking differently than I had ever hoped or imagined.

It was here that I cried out to God in a whole new way. Not with my usual, *"why me?"* but instead by asking, *"If not this, then what?"* Direction and purpose—these two things are what I was longing for. I wanted assurance from the Lord that my life had meaning just as I was: without children. You see, I had always felt it was expected of me to have children, to raise a family, and to live a life that appeared normal in societal ways. The disappointment of not having children was a daily weight, further pressed upon when others would comment on it.

Yet here I was, edging closer to the pivotal age of forty, when a sense of apprehension shadowed my steps. This wasn't just another birthday; it felt like a silent witness to the storms I'd weathered and the quiet victories I'd claimed along the way. I found myself dreading every day that inched closer to me having to accept that I was no longer in my thirties.

Despite past disappointments surrounding my birthdays, I was determined that this year would be different. Early in the year I had planned a bucket list trip. I wanted to go camping in Cherokee, North Carolina, and play Tribal Bingo.

I know this may seem like an odd thing to want to do as a bucket list trip, but I can assure you that this area and Bingo Hall held deep significance to me and my family. With a quiet longing for understanding, I hoped this visit would give meaning to my existence. I also hoped it would help me to unplug and seek the Lord for clarity on why my life didn't look how I envisioned it as a little girl playing with her dollhouse.

Mike and I had set our sights on the mountains and secured a cozy cabin for our getaway—and we weren't alone. Over dinner with some friends, prior to our departure, we shared our excitement with them. To our surprise, their enthusiasm matched ours, and suddenly, we were orchestrating a weekend retreat for four.

Mike and I arrived a day ahead of the others after navigating the wildest ride down a mountain on a curvy road through trees until finally we reached our destination. Instantly, I could see why this area was significant to my family. Walking up to our cabin, I was met with a beautiful stream and trees all around. The views were breathtaking from the front porch of the cabin, and it was extremely quiet and peaceful.

Surrender it All

Here I sat, gazing out across the beautiful landscape pouring my heart out to the Lord. Questioning, if my only true worth in this life was to have children and I couldn't physically have children, does that mean I'm worthless or that my life has no meaning? I carried so much guilt from being broken that I often couldn't look others in the eye when discussion of babies came up, and the mere act of holding a newborn baby made me physically ill as it was a reminder of what I couldn't have.

However, at this stage in my life I no longer searched for the answer to *why* I couldn't have children; rather, I searched for the answer to what I should be doing with my life that pleases God, children or not. I made a promise to God right then and there on that porch that I would open my heart and listen: *Wherever you lead, Lord, I will follow.*

Looking up through tears I watched as the sun broke through the trees casting a ray of light over the water. Such beauty to behold. I picked up my phone and began taking pictures. I knew I needed to capture what I was witnessing. I could feel God all around me as I watched the sun glisten in the water, swirling around the rocks and the water flowed downstream. This picture of God's beauty is still my screensaver on my phone today as a reminder of this moment in time—the moment I surrendered this part of my story to God once and for all. It was this ray of light piercing the darkness as I sat at the bottom of the ocean that caused me to begin the daunting task of attempting to free the anchors chain, desperate to rise to surface. This day, I accepted His design for my life, letting go of my own, stepping aside allowing Him to take the lead once again.

The rest of the trip was wonderful, I am certain that the right people joined us on that trip because they made our experience one that I will never forget. I am forever grateful for the memories made and the stories shared with each of them. It helped turning forty easier and opened my eyes in ways they had never been opened before. I cried a lot on this getaway. With each stone that was overturned and each lesson building upon the next, I left Cherokee a changed woman.

Obedience Brings Clarity

As I now reflect back on my time spent in those mountains, I came to terms with the reality that I may never experience motherhood in the traditional sense. Yet in this revelation, I discovered the birth of new ventures and ideas that have thrived and continue to enrich my life today. As unconventional as that may sound, I am content with where I am now because God brought me out of that grief and into a season of hope. My hope no longer lies in the prospect of becoming a mother; it now lies in knowing that God will guide me to those who need my help the most.

Have you ever felt like you didn't know exactly what to do or where to go with your life? When I was working through trying to figure it out on my own, my unclear direction caused me to feel frustrated with myself because I couldn't figure out what I should do. Some of what I have been through would often cause me to have clouded judgment, and I didn't trust that I would make the right decision on my own.

It's overwhelming to think about drastically shifting your life, to go from experiencing heartache to being hopeful isn't easy to do. If I'm being honest, I couldn't fully surrender my total control to God, I had to do it little by little until finally, I was ready to release it all. The moment I let go of the control I felt I had to have on figuring out my direction, peace entered in and clarity came forth. I knew the first step I had to take was to surrender and obey—this book is the outcome of my obedience.

Perhaps there is something you are holding onto as well, unable to trust that if you give up total control to God all will be right. When our faith is challenged during trials, it is natural for us to want to have full control over every situation we will encounter thereafter. But, if joy is what you seek, including God at the epicenter of all you do is the first step needed.

One thing that has brought me great joy in all of this is planning my next steps, but differently this time. God is at the center; He is guiding me on where to go next because I am giving Him the space to work within me through scripture and prayer. He can do the same for you, but only when you give Him the space to do it.

There is beauty to be found in God's design for our lives, but we must open our eyes to see it for what it is. That may feel impossible now for you, it's hard to see what is possible because what once was is no more. I encourage you to surrender it all to God, every ugly detail, leave nothing out, and tell Him how you feel. Don't fight back the tears, let them fall freely as you pour your heart out to God. Even though He already knows what you're going through, there is strength to be found at the feet of Jesus when we are our most vulnerable with Him. He wants us to speak it; He wants us to tell Him; He wants us to communicate with him openly and freely. Your path may not seem clear right now, but clarity comes when we are obedient.

Identity Struggle

It's natural to have goals and aspirations in life, but it's equally important to seek God's direction first. When I felt the need to be in control of my own life, I was filled with so much anxiety that it would often paralyze me in place, accomplishing nothing. I relied so heavily on what others thought I should do instead of leaning in and trusting God's direction for my life. In doing this, I was unsuccessful in my attempts and found myself farther away from my intended purpose.

When we take our eyes off Jesus standing in the middle of our path, guiding us forward, we end up making a detour. We wander blindly down rocky terrain as we try desperately to not fall flat on our faces while walking farther away from where we are supposed to be going. The result of this is a loss of purpose, direction, and, in some cases, loss of identity.

When we seek God's direction through His word and prayer first, we often find that He is taking us down a different road than we wanted to go, but the destination is more beautiful than we could ever imagine. Reminders pop up like lovely flowers along our path brightening our day with their beauty. The result of this is a sense of purpose, belonging, and knowing exactly who we are in Christ.

I wonder, are you in a place where you're trying to control your own destiny instead of obediently following God's path for you? You can let go today my friend; God is waiting with open arms.

Glimpses of Grace

Joseph's story in the Bible has always resonated deeply with me, causing me to reflect on the significance of trust and resilience. His journey from adversity to a place of significant influence—and ultimately saving countless lives—is a great example of faith and Godly guidance. As we dive into the pivotal moments of Joseph's life, detailed in Genesis chapters 37 to 50, I invite you to consider the ways in which trust, even in the toughest times, can lead to outcomes beyond our imagination. Let's read his story together:

So when Joseph came to his brothers, they stripped him of his robe— the ornate robe he was wearing— and they took him and threw him into the cistern. The cistern was empty; there was no water in it. As they sat down to eat their meal, they looked up and saw a caravan of Ishmaelites coming from Gilead. Their camels were loaded with spices, balm and myrrh, and they were on their way to take them down to Egypt. Judah said to his brothers, 'What will we gain if we kill our brother and cover up his blood? Come, let's sell him to the Ishmaelites and not lay our hands on him; after all, he is our brother, our own flesh and blood.' His brothers agreed. So when the Midianite merchants came by, his brothers pulled Joseph up out of the cistern and sold him for twenty shekels of silver to the Ishmaelites, who took him to Egypt. —Genesis 37:23–28

Grace is found when God protects Joseph by sparing him from death. Even though he was betrayed by his brothers, he did survive the exchange. Similarly, when we are faced with betrayal and disappointment, God protects us, giving us the strength to overcome the situation and keep going forward on our path. It is often difficult to see His protection when we are going through difficulties, if you are in a place now where it's impossible to see how any good can come out of your situation, ask God to give you strength and perspective today as you surrender it all to Him. Let's continue reading:

The Lord was with Joseph so that he prospered, and he lived in the house of his Egyptian master. When his master saw that the Lord was with him and that the Lord gave him success in everything he did, Joseph found favor in his eyes and became his attendant. Potiphar put him in charge of his household, and he entrusted to his care everything he owned. From the time he put him in charge of his household and of all that he owned, the Lord blessed the household of the Egyptian because of Joseph. The blessing of the Lord was on everything Potiphar had, both in the house and in the field. So Potiphar left everything he had in Joseph's care; with Joseph in charge, he did not concern himself with anything except the food he ate. —Genesis 39:2–6

Grace is found when God allows Joseph to find favor and success in his master's sight even during a time of slavery and hardship. Grace is also found when his master rewards him with responsibility and trust. We can find favor and success in God's sight when we are obedient and follow His guidance during our hardships. The best way to seek God's guidance is through studying the Bible and through honest prayer. Honest prayer, to me, is when we allow ourselves the freedom to be vulnerable with God. Are you angry? Tell Him, and then ask Him to soften that anger as you work your way back to Him. Watch how Joseph handled his anger:

> *Then Joseph said to his brothers, 'Come close to me.' When they had done so, he said, 'I am your brother Joseph, the one you sold into Egypt! And now, do not be distressed and do not be angry with yourselves for selling me here, because it was to save lives that God sent me ahead of you. For two years now there has been famine in the land, and for the next five years there will be no plowing and reaping. But God sent me ahead of you to preserve for you a remnant on earth and to save your lives by a great deliverance. So then, it was not you who sent me here, but God. He made me father to Pharaoh, lord of his entire household and ruler of all Egypt.* —Genesis 45:4–8

Grace is found in God's plan for Joseph. Despite the injustices Joseph faced, God's plan was at work leading to the preservation of life. Similarly, God's plan for our lives leads to the preservation of our lives and the lives of those we impact along the way. Just as I have been able to see God's hand in my journey, giving me a platform to help other women through hardships, I want you to imagine how you can use your hardships in a way that helps others through their own.

The Heart of the Matter: Trusting God's Design

Let's talk about what this means on our path to purpose. As we are walking on the straight path with Jesus guiding us, something or someone will inevitably cause us to stumble. That stumble can cause us to take our eyes off Jesus momentarily. As we pick ourselves back up, we wipe the dust off and we start again on our path even when we must approach the fork in the road before us. Sometimes we pick the one we feel is right, only to discover a rocky path has emerged.

When this happens, panic often sets in and while we can seek the Lord for guidance on what to do or where to go, we often still try to control the situation by running blindly through the rocks, only to fall flat on our face. I know this from personal experience as I have fallen flat on my face many times. It wasn't until I fully let go of the need to know my destination that I discovered the road leading me back to the path set forth by God. God doesn't promise His path will always be easy. He merely promises He will be with us every step of the way, over every bump, and with every fall.

Just because we find a straight path, doesn't necessarily mean we find all the answers. God reveals to us His plan in His timing, not in ours. How do we know the plan revealed is from God and not from ourselves? Is it biblical or of the world; is what you are doing pleasing to God?

Do not conform to the pattern of this world but be transformed by the renewing of your mind. Then you will be able to test and approve what God's will is—his good, pleasing and perfect will. —Romans 12:2

While I feel that God's plan for me is to write this book, I don't know what comes next, but I am trusting that He will reveal that to me as I go. This book has been an idea I've had and written for several years but have always found a way to disregard it, believing that no one would care about what I had to say. I didn't want to offend anyone with my Christian affiliation and would often keep silent and shy away from sharing my testimony. With each passing year, God would use a devotional I was studying or a conversation with a friend as a gentle reminder of the story I must share.

It's easy to get frustrated in the unknown, giving up control to God can leave us feeling uncertain about our future. As humans, we like stability, success, and recognition for our efforts. When we consider letting go of that, similar to looking down a path through a thick forest, we naturally wonder what's out there lurking in the darkness and are cautious as we step forward and hope for the best. Our paths are meant to lead us to a beautiful destination, but to arrive, we must first trust God.

Finding Joy

God understands your situation and your pain. He is here to show you a beautiful life that He has designed for you. Jesus said, *"I have told you these things, so that in me you may have peace. In this world you will have trouble. But take heart! I have overcome the world"* (John 16:33).

My friend, it's time to let go of your need to control the outcome and lean on God. Joy comes when we are patient and follow God's direction for us. There is a sense of freedom in letting go, as joy fills your heart, everything starts to line up in a way you never thought possible. Once you've begun to follow God's direction, pray that He sends a companion to join you, it's almost time for you to start letting people in again, I'll share more about this in the next chapter. You made it through the hardship and now, with God's help, you'll make it through the healing. Joy can be found when you invite God to join you on your journey.

Anchor Points

Rediscovering your authentic self and rebuilding your faith takes time. Be patient with yourself and trust that God will guide you through these exercises. Each exercise is meant to serve as an anchor point keeping you authentically anchored in Christ.

Affirm

Write the following scripture somewhere you will see it daily. Memorize it, and refer to it when you lose faith in who you are.

"Trust in the Lord with all your heart and lean not on your own understanding; in all your ways submit to him, and he will make your paths straight."—Proverbs 3:5–6

Prayer

Heavenly Father, thank you for reminding me that you have already paved the way for me. Life has been hard, I have been hurt and let down, and my path has been so very rocky and doesn't align with what I had hoped it would. I'm tired and frustrated, I feel like I'm not getting to where I need to be going, and I don't know what to do next. I give up my control to you, Lord, and humbly ask that you lead me down the path you have before me. Thank you, Lord, for the beauty that awaits me, Amen.

Journal Prompt

Spend some time in silence and reflect on your life leading to this moment in time.

Finish this sentence: *The path I've traveled up to this point looks like…*

Declaration Statements

"I am" statement: Write a statement about who you feel you are in this very moment. *Example: I am on a detour.*

I am

_____

_____

"I hope to be" statement: Write a statement about who you hope to be by the end of this book. *Example: I hope to be able to see the beauty in God's design for my life.*

I hope to be

_____

_____

Chapter Five
Rebuilding Friendship

We've journeyed from the bottom of the ocean to a new beginning, where we've found ourselves on solid ground once again. Now, we can begin to incorporate new habits as we draw closer to God. Despite the weight of our trials, there is hope found in connections made with others. After three months in solitude, I feared my friendships may have weakened. But as I longed for their company, I trusted in the security our deep roots had created.

In the wake of my miscarriage, I chose to share this deeply personal loss with only a handful of trusted individuals. My intention wasn't to seek answers or draw attention to my grief; it was to share my burden with those I believed could handle the fragility of my situation. This was the season I spent much of my time feeling as though I was submerged at the bottom of the ocean. I was desperate to find a lifeline to help pull me to the surface but with no luck. The discomfort my confession caused some individuals I shared with only reinforced a sobering reality: the topic of miscarriage remains a difficult one, often carried in silence by many women for this very reason. While Mike remained supportive, I was longing for a girlfriend I could open up to.

I hesitated to share my pain, fearing it might unsettle others. I struggled with the heavy silence that suppressed my loss. Retreating to my familiar coping mechanism, I chose solitude over vulnerability, burying my sorrow deep within. This introversion became a way of life, a learned survival tactic that favored isolation over the risk of exposing my raw wounds to the world. Through years of navigating life's hardships, I had created a solitary path, processing grief and hardship in the quiet recesses of my heart, far from the supportive embrace of shared understanding.

The sole tribute to our loss was found in the naming of my business—Lilian Grace Designs—in honor of the little life we had just lost. While it was too soon to know the gender of the baby, Mike and I had conversations prior about what our potential children's names would be and that was one we had picked for a daughter.

I hoped that by naming the business after Lilian Grace I would remain eager to nurture and help the business grow, giving me a reason to rise each day and celebrate its growth as one might a child's milestones. My business focused on building friendships from the heart, particularly in offering support during hardships, and the more I worked on my business, the more I felt closer to fulfilling my purpose to help others form deep-rooted friendships.

The year 2020 was one of my toughest years in business yet, as it was for so many others. It was during this time I came to appreciate how deeply I needed friendship in my life. During the global shutdown of 2020, my closest friend and I agreed to meet every Monday on video chat to check in with each other and combat the loneliness that came with being unable to see each other in person. These sessions became a lifeline, allowing us to share heart-to-heart conversations we'd never ventured into before.

This period of reflection revealed my weaknesses in the way I handled my friendships and my reluctance to share my vulnerabilities. I found myself sharing openly with my friend in a way I had never dared before, which felt both frightening and freeing. I could now see where I had closed myself off to friendships in the past prompting a reevaluation of my relationships and the efforts needed to fortify them in uncertain times.

I discovered the strength of enduring deeply rooted friendships—those rare bonds that stand the test of time. My friend became a constant in my life during this very challenging season. Whenever one of us struggled, we worked together to find solutions helping us get back on track. She became my *person*, a true "soul friend" who hears what I'm saying even when I'm silent. To this day, she still knows what to say to help me stand firmly in place like a tree with deep roots.

Like two friends with deep roots, when you individually root yourself in Christ, you form a deep-rooted relationship between yourself and Him. This is exemplified in Colossians where we read, *"So then, just as you received Christ Jesus as Lord, continue to live your lives in him, rooted and built up in him, strengthened in the faith as you were taught, and overflowing with thankfulness"* (Colossians 2:6–7).

The concept of friendship with roots running deep underground, intertwined and steadfast, serves as security amidst the storms of life. Such friendships are cultivated over time, with love and nurturing as the two of you work together to water and prune the tree as it grows. Establishing clear boundaries respects the time and energy of everyone, preventing emotional exhaustion while providing valuable nutrients in the form of encouragement. We are not meant to live life alone. I believe that when we are brave enough to let someone into the depths of our hearts, we will find a kindred spirit we hoped for.

If you have not yet found your person—that deep, meaningful friendship you've been hoping for—draw near to God and pray. Ask Him to prepare your heart for the day your paths cross so you can be the supportive, encouraging friend they need and be encouraged by them as well.

The Secret to Deep-Rooted Friendships

Wanting to understand the importance of friendship in my life, I sat down and drew a tree toward the top of my paper with a line indicating the ground. I left space under the line for roots where I wrote a characteristic of genuine friendship that came to mind. Words like trustful, accepting, loyal, genuine, loving, supportive, understanding, and more filled below the tree. As I read each of the words I had written, I wondered which of these characteristics was I bringing to my friendships?

What I uncovered is that the secret to deep-rooted relationships wasn't in the other person and how they treated me, but instead, it was within me and how I was showing up for them. I had to face the reality of my shortcomings and accept that I was an imperfect person with life problems that often spilled into my friendships. I was exhausting them with my negative thinking and constant need to complain. Once I confronted these vulnerabilities within me, I knew I needed to work on becoming a better person, for them and me.

As we all know, change doesn't happen overnight; it takes discipline and consistency to see change occur. I didn't want to make a big deal out of my revelation to them, so instead of talking about me, I challenged myself to listen to them more, to let them have space that I often dominated, and to offer them encouragement and challenges for personal growth. I had to remove all feelings of competition from the equation and celebrate their wins with them.

What I found when I did this was that I saw my friends in a whole new light, I learned more about them, my connection to them grew deeper, and I was suddenly vulnerable with them again. Joy began to be more present in our interactions with each other, and I found I was more at peace, content with the way the friendship was going, and free to be me without fear of rejection. I have rebuilt my friendships.

Rebuild Your Life with Friends

If you are reading this and you can't find who your friends are, I want to encourage you to pray for God's guidance and direction in this. Ask Him to reveal to you the faces and names of those in your life whom He wants you to create a connection with. Pray that He puts someone in your path that you connect with early on, that you can nurture and grow into a deep-rooted relationship. And as you wait, I invite you to begin working on establishing those characteristics within you that you hope to receive in someone else.

What does it look like to find a friend to celebrate life with as you're rebuilding after traumatic life events? For me, I am so thankful for the friends God has blessed me with after everything I have walked through. During some of my darkest seasons these sisters would reach out daily.

I'd like to share some ways that having close friends—or finding new ones—can significantly cultivate your path to rebuilding your life. Understanding that each person's journey to form meaningful friendships varies greatly, I've outlined a range of strategies to consider, tailored to diverse needs and circumstances.

1. **Online Groups:** Join existing groups or create a new one and invite in people you know and ask them to bring a friend.

In 2016 shortly after we said goodbye to our foster placement, I realized I had inadvertently pushed most of my friends away while I was focusing on my new family. Suddenly, I needed to be surrounded by people I could connect with for companionship as I processed the grief that came with a failed adoption.

I was not comfortable yet with in person dialogue and decided to form a social media group where I invited friends to join and invite others they knew who all had the same goal—forming friendships.

My amazing friends who have joined me consistently since then have spread love, joy, and support to one another. Watching their friendships form, grow, and flourish has been an amazing blessing to me, and I'm so grateful for each of them and their big hearts. They have taught me to be, do, and love better, without expecting anything in return.

2. **Prayer Partner:** Finding one person who shares similar beliefs as you and joining in together in daily devotions and prayer helps keep you anchored in Christ while forming a stronger bond with your friend.

I want to encourage you to find one person who shares the same faith as you and ask that person if they would be interested in studying daily devotions together with you that you could discuss. You can do this as simple as using a free app on your phone and taking turns picking a devotion to study or by each of you ordering a paperback devotional that you fill out and share photos of your answers in either a text or social media message. As you get to know her, you'll also get to know God's word more and more with each passing day as your roots of friendship grow deeper and deeper.

3. **Soul Friend:** Develop a friendship with roots that run deep and can withstand any trials that may come.

Perhaps what you need is more. You could have already worked through the first three solutions to friendship and find you are still searching for something more. Finding a soul friend is when you find someone you connect with on the deepest level possible; they recognize we all have shortcomings and keep no record of your wrongdoings. The two of you connect in a way that fits so well together the only explanation to this phenomenon is that you are intertwined in a way that God has placed you both together with a purpose in mind. How do you know you've reached this level of friendship? You feel it. If you do not yet have a soul friend, I encourage you to pray that God sends you one, because this level of friendship is a rare gem that everyone should have the joy of experiencing.

Part of rebuilding is also letting go of control over your friendships and allowing God to direct your connections. I must understand that if I am choosing to live my life authentically in a way that defines who I am to my core, I have to also let my friends live their lives authentically and trust that my heart is in good hands. Additionally, if deep-rooted relationships were my ultimate goal, I knew I also had to start putting them ahead of my selfish tendencies and give them the space they needed to lean on me for support.

Boundaries

Healthy friendships thrive on balanced boundaries with mutual respect and understanding. Your boundaries should be clear, consistent, and respectful to help establish transparent communication. Establishing these boundaries early on strengthens the friendships roots, offering security in navigating life's challenges together. Don't be afraid to have a conversation about boundaries with your friend, but make sure that it is at a time when you both have a clear mind and an open heart to be able to freely discuss the needs of each other.

Here are some examples of boundaries that I have incorporated into my friendships:

- A good friendship has a healthy balance of give and take—the boundary established to help you achieve this would be to practice taking turns speaking and before ending your conversation asking each other if there is any more they wish to share.

- Communication availability looks different for everyone based on their work and family schedules. Work together to pick a consistent day and time to check in with each other as often as you both can.

- Before offloading your thoughts on each other, first check in to make sure that now is a good time to discuss heavy topics. This helps ensure that communication lines are wide open and that both of you are able to work through the issues at hand.

- Respecting each other's beliefs is important to maintain a lasting friendship. One area you'll need to spend time in prayer is in choosing friends whose beliefs may not align with yours. If you are open to a friendship with someone of different beliefs, it is important to discuss the boundaries you both have around this topic early on and how you will address any faith related debates that may arise.

- Time spent apart after a disagreement often varies and a long period of silence may give off the impression that your friendship has ended. Setting up a time to check back in after there has been an argument helps to know when you can reach back out to her, or she can reach back out to you. Discuss a length of time that is acceptable for you both to process the disagreement alone before reconnecting to discuss.

Identity Struggle

Often, we are taught that if we are in a friendship that is one sided we should end it and move on to someone who reciprocates. What we see as a result is a series of short lived friendships that are not strong enough to withstand trials of any kind. I personally felt that if God was commanding me to love one another as Jesus loved me, I owed it to my friends to keep trying instead of giving up on them. What I found in this approach was that they were struggling in private with a hardship they were facing alone because they didn't trust that I could be their support system during their time of need due to my own situation. This sobering reality was the wakeup call I needed to be there for my friends when they needed me by being more present with them more frequently.

How many times do we push others away from us even if God brought them to us?

Glimpses of Grace

When we talk about relationships, we can learn from the story of Ruth as she is the prime example of putting others before her. Her whole story can be read in the book of Ruth, but I want to focus on finding where grace can be found in a couple of instances. Let's look at Ruth's story together:

> But Ruth replied, 'Don't urge me to leave you or to turn back from you. Where you go I will go, and where you stay I will stay. Your people will be my people and your God my God. Where you die I will die, and there I will be buried. May the Lord deal with me, be it ever so severely, if even death separates you and me.' When Naomi realized that Ruth was determined to go with her, she stopped urging her. —Ruth 1:16–18

Grace is found in Ruth's character. Her commitment to her mother-in-law is an act of companionship and loyalty. She was determined she would never leave Naomi's side. When times get tough, it is easy for us to leave our friend's side. It is in these moments we should dare to be more like Ruth, dig in our heels, and stay to help:

> *Boaz replied, 'I've been told all about what you have done for your mother-in-law since the death of your husband—how you left your father and mother and your homeland and came to live with a people you did not know before. May the Lord repay you for what you have done. May you be richly rewarded by the Lord, the God of Israel, under whose wings you have come to take refuge.'* —Ruth 2:11–12

Grace is found first in Naomi acknowledging the kindness Ruth has offered her in her selflessness and commitment. Grace is also found when Boaz praises Ruth for her kindness and prays that God will reward her for all she has done. Much like the rewards Ruth received for her kindness, our Father will reward us for loving our neighbor and sharing kindness with them. This alone should be enough for us to choose to be there for others without expecting anything in return.

The Heart of the Matter: The Power of Authentic Friendships

Authenticity is important in friendship. We should always strive to create a safe environment for others to feel as though they can be themselves near us, just as we want them to do the same for us. Acceptance of each other's authenticity is also important in friendship. When we share a sacred space of vulnerability, we make sure that boundaries are set in place prior. Each person should know the expectation held by one another in keeping vulnerabilities between the two of you. Some ways that you can be authentic within your relationship are to listen, be honest, take responsibility for your actions, treat your friend well, be present, or express yourself.

Having healthy boundaries established early in the friendship gives you both a guideline to follow to help keep the relationship intact. Is this a perfect process? Not always. What you'll find is we all grow in different directions. Part of fully accepting the other person is forgiving them for their transgressions against you. This doesn't mean that they'll remain in your life, some transgressions are irreparable, but even in those instances, forgiveness is important for you to continue moving ahead.

Finding Joy

Supportive relationships can provide companionship, acceptance, encouragement, and strength in challenging times. Nurture your friendships often and provide a safe space for them to be vulnerable with you. If God hasn't yet brought you friends who are here to walk beside you, pray diligently for a friend to be made known to you. Don't lose heart; for even if you feel alone in this moment, know that I am here beside you now as you journey through this book. You are not alone.

There is joy in discovering the qualities you possess that are an asset to your relationship. Take time to discover these qualities and ask God to help you define areas you feel need improved upon to develop deep-rooted relationships with others and open up new opportunities to meet someone you can connect with. Another common ground in finding a friend is to look into others who share a similar passion or hobby; I'll talk more about finding your passions in the next chapter. Joy is found when you allow God to bring a deep-rooted friendship into your life.

Anchor Points

Rediscovering your authentic self and rebuilding your faith takes time. Be patient with yourself and trust that God will guide you through these exercises. Each exercise is meant to serve as an anchor point keeping you authentically anchored in Christ.

Affirm

Write the following scripture somewhere you will see it daily. Memorize it, and refer to it when you lose faith in who you are.

"Therefore encourage one another and build each other up, just as in fact you are doing." —1 Thessalonians 5:11

Prayer

Heavenly Father, thank you for helping me discover the vulnerabilities in friendship I carry with me. I realize I may have kept my friends at arms length apart to guard my heart, and I ask that you help me to learn to let them in again. I pray, Lord, for my person, that you make them known to me and help me to nurture and grow that relationship into a deep-rooted relationship that lasts for a very long time. Thank you, Lord, for the friendship that awaits me, Amen.

Journal Prompt

The key to deep-rooted relationships begins with who we are authentically, including the vulnerable parts.

Complete this sentence: *The vulnerabilities I have that I need to address are...*

_____

_____

_____

_____

_____

_____

_____

_____

_____

_____

Declaration Statements

"I am" statement: Write a statement about who you feel you are in this very moment. *Example: I am a good friend.*

I am

_____

_____

"I hope to be" statement: Write a statement about who you hope to be by the end of this book. *Example: I hope to be a compassionate friend.*

I hope to be

_____

_____

Chapter Six

Rediscover Your Passions

When trying to get our footing on solid ground again, another important factor in your healing journey is in rediscovering your passions. For me, art and creativity are something I grew up appreciating and enjoying that were passed down to me by two generations. I learned about print press operators, where plates were used to capture the details in ink as the paper was fed through, and creating things like cereal boxes and game boards. I also learned the importance of CMYK *(Cyan, Magenta, Yellow, and Key Inks)* printing as the world evolved and the printing industry changed with it.

As a child, I would play "office" with misprinted forms that had carbon paper inserts and wrap presents using the roll butts of wrapping paper that had been printed and cut off the roll. I enjoyed giving both unwanted items a sense of repurposing and saving them from their fate of being discarded for being different. Early on, I had an imagination bigger than I was that allowed me the chance to explore and tap into my creative side by engaging in activities that involved art. While I didn't receive the gift of being a professional artist who could draw or paint beautiful pictures, I did have fun trying to work on becoming a better artist overtime.

I still love the smell of ink on paper. It brings me a sense of familiarity and safety, reminding me of home. There once was a time when I would hand-make greeting cards and stationery using rubber stamps and ink pads to sell at craft shows. I would spend hours cutting, stamping, and gluing cards to either swap with other makers or sell at local craft shows. As time progressed and the world continued to evolve, I sought to learn new techniques for bringing my designs to life.

This craving for creativity led me to photography when Mike and I first started dating, where I spent seven years behind the camera. I took photographs of landscapes, animals, babies, weddings, parties, people, and even once at a famous country music singer's concert to capture memories through my lens of John Conlee on stage and off. It was truly a "pinch me" moment when I was introduced to him, but the best part was the honor of being there and the memories that were made.

During my time in photography, I learned valuable skills in digital imagery through classes along with trial and error. I quickly discovered my style preferences when it came to editing photos and found that my favorite part was putting together a photo book for my clients with some of the best images I had taken. This road ignited a passion for graphic design leading me to enroll in online classes putting my skills to the test while our foster children were at school.

After losing our foster placement, I struggled to find joy in picking up the camera once more. Due to grief and lack of time from working overtime hours at the job I had taken then, I ended up setting everything aside for quite some time. I did try to find a hobby that worked for me and worked with my schedule, things like gardening, coloring, crafting, and even painting. I debated on getting back into one of my earlier passions from early adulthood of community theatre and came close as I tried to muster up the courage to attend a meeting at a local playhouse; however, I lacked the bravery needed to follow through with it.

Because of the trauma I had faced, I tried hard to tap into my inner child and do all the different things that used to make me happy as a child when I was creative. I wanted to wake her up inside of me with permission to be messy and create. I wanted to take the paint that lay before me and turn it into a masterpiece that made me smile. I was desperate to find something, anything really, that could bring me out of the despair I constantly felt. Unfortunately, it was difficult to rediscover that part of me because I was still sad all the time.

This led to one of the most creative moments yet. What if I could approach this process differently? What if I gave myself permission to dream of a place where my hobby and business could coexist in harmony? I grabbed a sheet of paper and a pen and began a mind map of whatever came to mind about the possibility. My pen flowed as quickly as my brain processed memories, even things that I remembered as a child. Perhaps the creative part of me was still inside of me waiting to be awoken after all.

As I took a step back and read over my mind map, I could see a glimmer of hope in the possibilities that were before me. I smiled at a familiar thought—growing up helping my family at craft events where everything on display made sense and went together. They looked beautiful next to each other, and I listened as customers complimented on the display. I knew early on in my business planning that I wanted to be more than a hobby crafter. I also wanted to help others feel valued, cherished, and loved by creating an experience that made others remember me because they felt the impact. I needed a creative outlet to express what I was feeling and experiencing while simultaneously helping others. The thought of combining the two made the most sense to me, but I didn't know where to begin.

No matter what I did, I found this didn't quite have the same impact as graphic design did which only led to my curiosity more. I also liked creative writing and was exploring ways to combine these. My business was still very new at the time, and these hobbies lent well when paired together to help me come up with new ideas for product design, but because I lacked clarity in which direction I should go, I ended up with a table full of products that—you guessed it—didn't make sense.

Focus on What Lights You Up

When we are faced with too many decisions, it can go one way or the other. We either freeze in place, doing nothing, or we take that first step. I challenged myself to do the latter, act and figure it out as I went along. I became a sponge, soaking up all the knowledge I could find on graphic design—color psychology, textures, typography, layout, composition. The list was endless.

This leads me to a question for you, my friend: What is something you've done that causes you to light up? Think about trying it again to see if it still had the same effect on you. Or maybe it's something new where you need to simply take a step forward and give it a shot. In the same way I challenged myself, I want to issue a challenge to you: Become a sponge, soak up knowledge in the area of your passions, and give it a shot.

Another action I took was to equip myself with the tools needed to create everything I wanted to create while still adding to my list as time progressed and my skills began to grow. While hobbies can be expensive, a way around this expense that I found was during the holidays when friends or family would ask for gift ideas. I shared my unique wish list of items that would help me develop my skills and provide me with resources that would serve me well into the future. This is a simple way for you to begin collecting the tools you'll need to be successful.

Another shift I needed to make was in my mindset. I realized I didn't need to be an instant expert at what I was attempting to do. As I tried to learn and organize everything on my own, I often became overwhelmed, and to combat this, I decided to try drawing digitally to disconnect my mind. I am not someone who can draw beautifully on paper, let alone digitally. What I found, however, was I enjoy angry sketching on days when life feels hard. I grab my digital tablet and pen, and I sit outside while I draw angry sketches and scribbles. At first, it was a jumbled mess, but I learned how to control the pen flow and pressure to be able to use it in a way that produces fun drawings. I now use some on my products and my branding.

Sketching is the hobby I found that lit me up and challenged me to pursue graphic design as my career because it brings me so much joy. When we focus on what lights us up, we may uncover a new path to take that leads us to a much brighter destination.

Mindset is Everything

The massive mindset shift that has occurred within me because of rediscovering my passions happened over time and with consistently practicing for over two years. It didn't happen the first time I tried to design, or even the hundredth time. To be honest, it didn't happen until, suddenly, everything clicked.

As I was just starting in design and trying to pave my path in the graphic design world, I was criticized, sometimes harshly, by colleagues. Now that I was finally brave enough to step out and try something new after going through such an incredible loss, it seemed as though my toughest critics had something to say about it. Because I was in such a fragile place, I allowed those criticisms to slow my progress down. I let them win. I went through a season of creativity block where no matter what I designed; I hated it. My mindset was at an all-time low during that drought and threatened to destroy everything I had worked so hard to build.

I knew that if I wanted to let my creativity flow again, I would have to dig deeper into what God says we should do with our gifts. I began asking myself the questions that made me uncomfortable, like why do you feel this is what you are supposed to be doing? I forced myself to answer honestly and without hesitation that I was created with this purpose in mind to design beautiful graphics for others who need it and to bring joy and hope in the lives of all I cross paths with, as ordained by God.

Once I accepted this truth as mine, I then began to pray that God would open the doors He wanted me to walk through so that I could honor Him with design. Once I prayed for open doors, I continued to work hard at perfecting my skills. I knew that to achieve success I had to work for it.

Determination and focusing on your passions produce success. On days when you feel like quitting or shifting your focus, I invite you to reconsider. Pray about it, seek direction through God's word and prayer, pick yourself up, and try again. As time progresses, you'll change into the woman that God designed you to be. Take what you are passionate about and use your gifts to honor God the best way you know how.

I know this to be true because it is what has happened to me. I believe that everyone deserves beautiful branding, which is why I offer my design services in a variety of ways to help other business owners capture their brand identity in a way that is unique to them.

Just as I create each design to be authentic for the client who hired me to make it, God has authentically created each of us, equipping us with gifts that are ours to use according to His good and perfect will. We can uncover our spiritual gifts when we are authentically anchored in Christ and give Him the chance to reveal to us what they are by prayer and study of His word.

Identity Struggle

My friend, when we lose our sense of identity and purpose, it is difficult to discover what hobbies or passions bring joy to our lives. Having child-like faith can also be considered when choosing a hobby or activity you love that will help you become your true authentic self. Opening ourselves to explore hobbies in a similar manner as a child permits us to let go of controlling what we are doing and embrace playfulness.

When you find activities that bring you joy, do them on days that feel heavy and hard. Sometimes it's as simple as coloring in a coloring book or writing in your journal while you sit outdoors. Other times, you may discover a talent deep within that God has equipped you with. I encourage you to lean into your inner child and not let fear stop you from trying new things.

Have you found yourself shying away from exploring a hobby or a passion for fear of failure? My friend, God is with you to reignite that passion today.

Glimpses of Grace

As we discover these hidden talents, we didn't realize they were there or they were forgotten. We are encouraged to use our gifts for good to help others who, like us, are struggling. In 1 Samuel chapter 16, we hear of a story of Saul, who is struggling in darkness and needs someone to help him see the light. If David had not leaned into his gifts of playing the lyre, Saul's story could have ended poorly earlier on. Let's look to scripture for more:

Now the Spirit of the Lord had departed from Saul, and an evil spirit from the Lord tormented him. Saul's attendants said to him, 'See, an evil spirit from God is tormenting you. Let our lord command his servants here to search for someone who can play the lyre. He will play when the evil spirit from God comes on you, and you will feel better.' So Saul said to his attendants, 'Find someone who plays well and bring him to me.' —1 Samuel 16:14–17

Grace is found in the remedy to Saul's distress. God provided the remedy by placing the thought on the attendant's heart to have someone play the lyre to help him. Much like Saul finding a remedy, we too, can find a remedy in exploring our passions closer to determine where God is pointing you to use your gifts to potentially bring joy to someone.

One of the servants answered, 'I have seen a son of Jesse of Bethlehem who knows how to play the lyre. He is a brave man and a warrior. He speaks well and is a fine-looking man. And the Lord is with him.' Then Saul sent messengers to Jesse and said, 'Send me your son David, who is with the sheep.' So Jesse took a donkey loaded with bread, a skin of wine and a young goat and sent them with his son David to Saul. —1 Samuel 16:18–20

Grace is found in the gifts given to David by God to play the lyre and in his braveness. God has chosen David for this specific purpose, that he may go to Saul. Much like David, God has chosen you for a specific purpose. You may already know it in your heart but have long given up on the thought or idea; or, you may not yet have uncovered what your purpose is. God is instilling braveness in you now so that you can choose to discover your potential, leading to uncovering your authenticity.

David came to Saul and entered his service. Saul liked him very much, and David became one of his armor-bearers. Then Saul sent word to Jesse, saying, 'Allow David to remain in my service, for I am pleased with him.' Whenever the spirit from God came on Saul, David would take up his lyre and play. Then relief would come to Saul; he would feel better, and the evil spirit would leave him. —1 Samuel 16:21–23

Grace is found when David finds favor with Saul. Saul likes David and is pleased with him to the extent that he wants David to remain in service to him. Grace is also found when David plays his lyre, relief would come to Saul, causing the evil spirit to leave him. Much like David finding favor with Saul for using his gifts to serve, we also can find favor in God when we use our gifts to glorify Christ. God brings relief to those He puts in our path that needs our gifts and services. If we choose to do nothing, we serve no one, but if we choose to step out in faith and help someone, we will have done our very best to bring relief to someone who feels as if they are drowning. By being obedient and serving others in a way that God has gifted me to do, it brings me great joy to help where I am needed while also doing something I love.

The Heart of the Matter: Childlike Faith

When I face hardships that keep me from experiencing joy in the things I once loved, I have found it takes a lot more of my effort to muster up the courage to try again. It often seems easier to say "no" and sit with our pain than to challenge ourselves to do the things that once made us happy. When your life doesn't look like what you envisioned it would, your first instinct may be to just quit trying. The enemy seeks to kill and destroy all joy that remains within us by attacking the very things we love. It takes one simple action to change from defeated to hopeful, all you have to do is try until you find something that works.

I remember picking up a paintbrush and staring at a blank canvas for a few minutes before getting angry, slamming the brush down on the table, and walking away. My anger at that moment surprised me. I don't know why it made me angry other than I couldn't think of what to paint because I had put an expectation on myself that whatever I did paint had to be perfect. It wasn't until I permitted myself to digitally scribble color on a canvas with no boundaries—the only expectation that there should be no white remaining—that I finally allowed my inner child free from captivity. I'll admit, it was the ugliest drawing I've ever done, but I laughed a loud and hard laughter emitting from my belly as it shook my shoulders. I laughed so hard tears fell down my face. My inner child was free.

Perhaps art isn't your passion, but whatever brings you joy, I invite you to explore that with no boundaries or expectations of yourself. Permit yourself to approach this process as a child does when they first learn a new skill. Be honest with yourself and with God as you try. Will you fail? Maybe, but every time we try again, we only improve and eventually will master the skill when we are brave enough to keep trying—which sounds like success to me.

Finding Joy

I have found rediscovering your passions as a powerful motivator for healing and self-discovery. When everything has been stripped away from us and we are in a season of rebuilding, it's a good time to revisit the things we put on the back burner that used to bring us joy. I'm so grateful I challenged myself to lean into my passion for design because when it came time for a sudden pivot, I was able to work through the overwhelm by disconnecting from the situation and redirecting my focus. I'll share more about what to do when we are forced to pivot in the next chapter.

Even though you may be a different person today than you were when you enjoyed your hobbies, there is still something to be found that sparked joy in you—that something is worth exploring again. If revisiting something you used to do brings more pain with it or it feels too overwhelming to do again, challenge yourself to try something new that you've always wanted to do. Someday can be today if you simply start right now. Joy can be found when we break our inner child free from the shackles that hide her.

Anchor Points

Rediscovering your authentic self and rebuilding your faith takes time. Be patient with yourself and trust that God will guide you through these exercises. Each exercise is meant to serve as an anchor point keeping you authentically anchored in Christ.

When it comes to rediscovering our passions, it's best to not overthink it and to be very fluid in our approach. When I wrote out my mind map, I wrote things as they came to mind, no matter how silly it seemed. Then, when I had written all that I could think of, I was able to go back and narrow it down. The important thing in all of this is to give space to allow God to work and direct you as you begin to uncover what is within.

Affirm

Write the following scripture somewhere you will see it daily. Memorize it, and refer to it when you lose faith in who you are.

"For we are God's handiwork, created in Christ Jesus to do good works, which God prepared in advance for us to do." —Ephesians 2:10

Prayer

Heavenly Father, thank you for reminding me of the things that once brought me joy. I ask, Lord, that you help me see what skills or gifts you have blessed me with. Please make known to me how you want me to use them to help someone else in need. I haven't always felt valuable, Lord, and I see now that I can and do bring value to those around me. I want to rediscover my passions in a new light, your light. Thank you, Lord, for the joy that awaits me, Amen.

Journal Prompt

The passions and/or hobbies I once had that brought me joy were...

_____

_____

_____

_____

_____

_____

_____

_____

_____

_____

_____

_____

_____

_____

_____

_____

_____

_____

_____

_____

_____

_____

_____

_____

_____

_____

_____

_____

_____

_____

_____

_____

Declaration Statements

"I am" statement: Write a statement about who you feel you are in this very moment. *Example: I am a graphic designer.*

I am

_____

_____

"I hope to be" statement: Write a statement about who you hope to be by the end of this book. *Example: I hope to be able to share my design skills with others to bring them joy while glorifying God.*

I hope to be

_____

_____

Chapter Seven
Forced to Pivot

My friend, you are making amazing progress. You've escaped the bottom of the ocean, swam to shore, rebuilt your friendships, and rediscovered your passion. Life is finally starting to look up again, and hope is being restored. It is in this moment the enemy will likely try to come swiftly to try and test your newly restored faith in God—by sending tidal waves through your life to see how you respond. Guard your heart, my friend, keep your eyes focused on Jesus, and know that God will use anything thrown at you now to help you pivot in a way that only serves you and Him better.

God was preparing me for a very specific moment back in 2020. In forced isolation, I took it upon myself to pour into my relationship with God more. I knew that I had been disobedient and had wandered far from God's mission for me, and my business. I had to learn what it was that I could do to get back on track. Unfortunately, it took me a little longer than I would have liked before I learned how to achieve inner peace and reduce the anxiety of running a business in a world that no longer looked or felt the same.

In my desperation to succeed, I turned my hobby into my career, leaving me without a creative outlet to refuel. I now had deadlines and had clients who I was designing for that were counting on my ability to maintain my creativity. The pressure kept building up as I had this need to prove I was successful. I had split my business model in two, confusing not only myself but also those who followed me. I had my greeting card and stationery brand that was doing well in stores, and I had my brand design services offered on a referral basis, neither of which was receiving my full attention.

After an unpleasant social media encounter with a follower, I allowed the enemy to dictate my path which led to the destruction of everything I had worked so hard to build. Critical feedback is often difficult to not take personally, and though I didn't know this person, I was humiliated by the comments made on my appearance in a live video I had done earlier that day. I took the comments to heart and even went as far as waitlisting my branding and design work so I could focus on product development for my stationery business. I'd love to say this was a smart business move, but the reality is, it only caused my self-esteem and lack of confidence to worsen. I was desperate for there to be a knock on a door of opportunity that could change the course of how I do everything.

An opportunity presented itself as I recalled a vivid memory from years past when I was attending a weekend retreat over my twenty-first birthday. It was the day before my birthday, and throughout the day, I was continually reminded of Revelation 3:20: *"Here I am! I stand at the door and knock. If anyone hears my voice and opens the door, I will come in and eat with that person, and they with me."* It was as if God was telling me that if I heard His voice and knocked at the door, I should open it. That evening, as we were winding down to go to sleep, there was a pounding and shouting on the other side of the door, and I stopped to speak through the locked door to whoever was outside in the darkness.

Desperation filled her voice in her brokenness. I could feel her fear and agony, but I couldn't open the door without a key. Another person was with me, and I asked her to find a leader while I remained speaking to the faceless voice on the other side of the door until someone from the retreat could bring her inside. We were instructed to go back to our sleeping area and get some rest for the night as they whisked her down the hall towards the offices. We were shielded from what happened to her, keeping her story safe within the clergy of the church, as it should be. The next day they told me I had helped her find safety that night, just by talking to her. This was when I decided never to question God again if He told me to answer a knock. This memory is now the catalyst to the biggest pivot I will have faced yet, changing how I do business to ensure it is more in alignment with God's vision.

Open the Door

As I am faced with unexpected twists or turns in life, I do my best not to view it as a "doom and gloom" situation anymore. I've come to understand that sometimes God clears away aspects of our lives that no longer align with serving Him, creating space for new opportunities that lie ahead. Holding onto what needs to end only delays the freedom and possibilities meant for us. This doesn't mean that whatever caused the pivot in our lives doesn't also cause us pain or sadness. It's okay to mourn the closing of a door just as it is okay to also rejoice in the opening of a new one.

For the last seven years I have carried my business as best I could until my current reality was telling me it was time to make a hard decision. It was a chilly fall day when I decided to go for a walk to clear my mind, but even after putting my shoes and jacket on, I found myself hiding behind the closed front door before me. For some reason I was scared to open it and step out onto the porch. Why? Likely because I knew that I needed to allocate some of my precious walk time sorting out the direction for my business.

Fear kept me standing there as I let my mind wander. I began remembering many years earlier when the two smiling faces stood before me beneath the tree in the front yard while I took fall pictures of the four of us for our Christmas cards. The tree was a constant reminder of *them*, my children, as I watched it grow while they were growing until suddenly, they were gone. Now, on the other side of the door stood a much taller tree casting shade across the front lawn as its colorful leaves drifted softly to the ground. These memories, while fleeting, still take my breath away.

Even though my walk held the promise of autumn's vibrant hues, the simple act of stepping outside suddenly seemed insurmountable. I wiped away the tears that had begun to trickle down my face and took a deep breath as I braced myself for the impact of stepping out onto the front porch to face the tree. I exhaled as I took in the beautiful sight before me, closed the door, and walked through the rustling leaves underneath the tree as I courageously began my walk and new journey in life.

On my walk I began to realize that change didn't have to be feared. Just as the weather changes, so do the seasons in our lives—this is natural. Admiring the leaves in our neighborhood that had begun turning a stunning shade of red and vibrant yellow just before falling to the ground, I felt peace in my heart that it was time for me to make a big change in my business. No matter how scared I was, I knew I had to stop running from God and start running to Him instead. This was the day I made my decision to stop hiding behind the scenes and take center stage of my business. When I got back from my walk, I committed to writing this book in November, which was only a month and a half away. I knew it would be difficult for me to be vulnerable, but all I could think about was the woman standing on the other side of the closed door, waiting on me.

Let Him In

My friend, I want to ask you: are you currently running from God? Maybe you've never questioned this before now because your faith has always been strong, or perhaps you're afraid to respond because the answer scares you. If I have learned anything it's that our faith is constantly being tested, it's common to trip and fall even when we are trying our best not to. This is precisely what makes us human: our imperfections. Our sin doesn't make God love us any less. He knows, *"for all have sinned and fallen short of the glory of God"* (Romans 3:23). He still loves us and wants us to confess our sins and continue trying to do better. *"If we confess our sins, he is faithful and just and will forgive us our sins and purify us from all unrighteousness."* (1 John 1:9)

Friends, God is knocking on the door of your heart right now. He's calling out to you. Will you let Him in?

Identity Struggle

In the journey to rediscover your authentic identity, one moment you may find yourself standing on the shore, gazing at the vast ocean, and in the next, you could be overwhelmed by a tidal wave, pulling you back to sea. I want to assure you this is all part of the process. These moments, they test our faith, tempting us to shift our gaze away from Jesus, leaving us wondering where our anchor has disappeared as we start to tread water once more. Yet, it's crucial that we do not let ourselves be overtaken by the currents of doubt.

The beautiful thing about a pivot is you can be safely anchored on shore and simply shift your direction from the point in which you currently are, but because it seems so frightening, we often forget we can ease into it when we are anchored in Christ. These pivots in life can often cause us to run away from God out of fear of the unknown. When life feels like it's finally going well and something happens to threaten the happiness we've only just uncovered, it often leaves us wondering why—what is the purpose? If we aren't careful, we may spend too much time paralyzed by fear, potentially missing the knock of opportunity on the other side of the door. It is important to remain vigilant. God calls out to us softly as He tries to show us He is in full control.

My friend, I want to challenge you: How many times do you find yourself fearful, focusing too much on the closed door that you end up missing what God is showing you on the other side?

Glimpses of Grace

When we are called by God but are thrown off course, we will find ourselves in trouble. A reminder of how disobedience can throw us off God's plan and wreak havoc in our lives is found in the story of Jonah. While I encourage you to read the book of Jonah in its entirety to fully capture the magnitude of disobedience in Jonah's life, I want to highlight a few passages below that I feel are helpful to us in our circumstances:

> From inside the fish Jonah prayed to the Lord his God. He said: "In my distress I called to the Lord, and he answered me. From deep in the realm of the dead I called for help, and you listened to my cry. You hurled me into the depths, into the very heart of the seas, and the currents swirled about me; all your waves and breakers swept over me. I said, 'I have been banished from your sight; yet I will look

again toward your holy temple.' The engulfing waters threatened me, the deep surrounded me; seaweed was wrapped around my head. To the roots of the mountains, I sank down; the earth beneath barred me in forever. But you, Lord my God, brought my life up from the pit. "When my life was ebbing away, I remembered you, Lord, and my prayer rose to you, to your holy temple. "Those who cling to worthless idols turn away from God's love for them. But I, with shouts of grateful praise, will sacrifice to you. What I have vowed I will make good. I will say, 'Salvation comes from the Lord.'" And the Lord commanded the fish, and it vomited Jonah onto dry land.—Jonah 2*

Grace can be found in God's mercy as He raises Jonah from the deep despite his disobedience and difficult circumstances. Much like Jonah, we often find ourselves in the pit of despair, often because we stray from what God is calling us to do. Sometimes we need to force a pivot in our lives by allowing God to place us back on track by surrendering to His leading. Trust that as He had mercy on Jonah, He will also have mercy on you in your situation:

Then the word of the Lord came to Jonah a second time: 'Go to the great city of Nineveh and proclaim to it the message I give you.' Jonah obeyed the word of the Lord and went to Nineveh. Now Nineveh was a very large city; it took three days to go through it.—Jonah 3:1–3

Grace is found when God gives Jonah a second chance by repeating the original command to go to Nineveh. Just because Jonah ran, didn't mean that God didn't want him to complete the task he was originally called to complete. Much like Jonah, we are also called to serve God in ways that are bigger than we dare dream of. Insecurities often stop us from answering the call because we fear what we do not know, so we run or hide.

My friend, God wants you to know that He is extending a second chance to you now. He has a purpose for you, and if you're honest with yourself, you're aware deep down in your heart what that purpose is; yet you fear obedience. I encourage you today to put fear aside and surrender to God's call. Once Jonah was obedient to God's call, we see Nineveh's people responding to his message with repentance (Jonah 3:4–10). There is someone out there, somewhere, who really needs you to be obedient to God's call so they too can repent and turn back to God.

The Heart of the Matter: Finding Purpose in Challenges

Let's talk about what it means when we find our purpose in unexpected challenges. In my own life, when a door closes unexpectedly, I tend to react with negativity instead of having an open mind to look at the big picture. I have been learning lately that when God closes a door, it's to open up our hearts more to prepare us to serve Him in ways we've only dreamed of.

My friend, I understand the fear you may be feeling right now; the notion of serving God and heeding His call might seem overwhelming, as if it's beyond your capacity and you doubt your ability to fulfill it. I've felt similarly about myself more often than I'd like to acknowledge. I've let those old labels resurface, picking them up and holding onto them as though their weight carries significance, instead of recognizing as they threaten to pull me under. I've been deemed unworthy, faced laughter, and endured doubts about my abilities from others.

But despite it all, I persevere. I know God is calling me; therefore, He must also be equipping me. Surely, He wouldn't bring me to this place and not give me the tools needed to follow His command. Just as he calls and equips me, He also does the same for you.

Finding Joy

Find strength in your ability to adapt and grow, guided by your unwavering faith in God. When we disobey God, unintentionally or otherwise, we can find ourselves back in deep waters living life on autopilot which we'll cover in the next chapter. Similarly, when we obey God, we can help others find their way back to shore, just as we have found ours. There is joy to be found in the "forced pivot", but to see it, we must first look to God.

When our faith hangs in the balance as the enemy threatens to extinguish all hope within us, we must make a decision that feels impossible. While it may seem easier to throw in the towel and let the enemy win, I want to remind you today that it's far more rewarding to put up a fight and defend your relationship with God.

You have a choice: depths of despair and destruction or a lifetime of growth and learning. When you find what brings you the most joy personally, you'll find your answer lies there. Joy is found when we discover that neither path is without obstacles, but one offers a helping hand.

Anchor Points

Rediscovering your authentic self and rebuilding your faith takes time. Be patient with yourself and trust that God will guide you through these exercises. Each one is meant to be an anchor point to help keep you authentically anchored in Christ.

Affirm

Write the following scripture somewhere you will see it daily. Memorize it, and refer to it when you lose faith in who you are.

> *"Here I am! I stand at the door and knock. If anyone hears my voice and opens the door, I will come in and eat with that person, and they with me."* —Revelations 3:20

Prayer

Heavenly Father, thank you for your patience in me and in my disobedience. It is never my intent to do the opposite of what you ask. Please help me, Lord, to have the strength and courage to go where you lead me. Lord, please quiet the noise within my mind so that I may hear your call at the door as you knock. Please give me the strength to open the door and step through it to what awaits me on the other side. Thank you, Lord, for believing in me when others haven't, Amen.

Journal Prompt

What is on the other side of the door that scares me?

_____

_____

_____

_____

_____

_____

_____

_____

_____

_____

_____

_____

_____

_____

_____

_____

_____

_____

Declaration Statements

"I am" statement: Write a statement about who you feel you are in this very moment. *Example: I am scared to walk through the door that awaits me.*

I am

_____

_____

"I hope to be" statement: Write a statement about who you hope to be by the end of this book. *Example: I hope to be a messenger for God.*

I hope to be

_____

_____

Chapter Eight

Autopilot

Two years after coming back to the shore, I thought that I had reached the point where I was able to start living life in a way that brought me happiness. I drew closer to God every day, I was working my dream job as a graphic designer, and Mike and I were discussing getting something that was on our wish list for a long time, an RV. So why did it feel like something was off?

Every day I followed the same routine: wake up to spend time in prayer and devotions, work all day with lunch at my desk while rushing to meet deadlines, have dinner and one TV show with Mike when he came home, work some more, and finally off to bed. My life was predictable, and there was no room for surprises or fun outings because every minute I had in free time I managed to turn into work time.

One day, as I was rushing through the house to get back to my office in time for a meeting, I found myself pausing in the living room to notice the paint on the walls was dim and chipped, crumbs were scattered on the counter and leading to the morning's dirty dishes—stacked and ready to wash. As I went to fill the dog's empty water dish, I caught the reflection of myself looking exhausted in the mirror hanging by the couch. But, I didn't have any more time to waste noticing the endless areas of my life that needed attention, I filled the dog bowl and then I raced up the stairs just in time to get signed into the meeting as I carried out my rinse and repeat schedule of the day.

When I turned off my computer for the evening, I noticed my closed planner sitting next to me and wondered when the last time was that I sat and planned out anything. I picked it up and flipped through it to discover that the last time I had used my planner was six months prior. That couldn't be right. I had always been a strict planner. I would spend every Monday morning mapping out my to-do list for the week and looking over my numbers from the previous week to ensure I was on target to reach my quarterly goals. Disappointed in myself, I closed the planner and tossed it back on my desk to head downstairs and prepare dinner.

As I washed the morning dishes and wiped down the counter, I noticed it was extremely silent in the house. Normally, while doing any type of cleaning or cooking activity, I would always play music to lift my mood, but this day was different…I felt different.

It was only later that evening, as I settled into the recliner and my attention was drawn back upon the weary walls of my living room, that I came to understand I had been navigating life on autopilot. The pile of magazines lying untouched on the coffee table, alongside my abandonment of any form of planning, served as stark indicators that this state of disengagement had persisted for at least six months, if not more. Grief has this way of weighing down every aspect of existence, extinguishing even the slightest desire to engage in activities that once filled me with joy, which was a troubling realization.

I challenged myself to look closer at the state my home was in. I walked from room to room, becoming more and more angry at myself for the chaotic messes I found. I used to be the person people would come to and ask for organization tips and help decluttering, but now it seemed I had fallen victim to my pain, allowing it to cause inattentiveness in my home. The cobwebs in the corners and dust bunnies accumulating on my home decor were a sign that I was no longer prioritizing my house. The reflection I saw in the mirror was another reality check that I had stopped caring for myself like I should be.

Oh, how I wish I could say that this realization alone sparked an immediate turnaround, that I could instantly rebound and find my way again. Yet, grief didn't adhere to such a straightforward path, and frankly, neither do I. Believing in overnight transformation is a fairy tale notion. Instead, I leaned into the very principles I teach, offering myself a measure of grace as I slipped into bed and pulled out my journal.

That night, I poured into my journal words that have recently resurfaced again, casting light on the chapter of life I was navigating back then. The feelings I was once again trying to understand led me to read the journal entries that were able to put words to emotions.

Encountering these words again transported me directly back to the emotions of that moment:

> I'm so exhausted—working too many hours. I am unable to serve anyone in this state. The enemy uses busyness as a way to stop us from fulfilling our mission in Christ. I am avoiding the truth...I am hiding behind my to-do list. I am not serving as I should be.

Woah. That entry cut me to my core when I found it, tears flooded my eyes again as I remembered the pain I held onto. I longed for a way out of the mundane lifestyle I was living. I assume you probably want to know how to go from living on autopilot to living a more purpose-filled life. While the answer to this is complex—in part because I'm still very much a work in progress—I'll do my best to share the path I've walked so you too can find your way forward.

Facing Reality

When we are living on autopilot, it can feel as if we are standing in the middle of a busy street where people are all around us traveling in different directions at different speeds. As we watch them pass us by, we feel nothing, no emotions come to mind, we are indifferent. What if what we see pass us by aren't people, but opportunities flying by us because we are too disconnected to notice what's ahead? We must break the cycle of being on autopilot as soon as we recognize we are living in it. *But how?*

It's great to want to change, but it's fantastic if we dare to take the needed steps toward change. For the first few days after my discovery that I was living my life on autopilot, I would tell myself that each day would be different, and that I would make changes, yet day after day kept slipping away, and more opportunities passed me by. Why? Because I was not yet in the right frame of mind to be able to make such a drastic lifestyle change, I knew I would have to find a way that would work for me and fit into my existing schedule.

I would make mental notes of things. I wanted to do projects I felt may help break my patterns—things like purging my closet, cleaning all the knick-knacks I have accumulated, and even painting the house. I made so many mental notes of things that needed to be done because they had been left undone for so long that I caused myself to enter a panic attack by bombarding myself with questions.

But what if I can't?

What if I'm not able?

What if nothing changes and I'm destined to fail at this too?

Sound familiar? This was the moment I realized that the trauma of feeling stuck in the ocean's depths still clung to me, and so I allowed myself to weep. Confronting my reality was intimidating, but I knew that acknowledging the need to break free from this autopilot existence was the first step towards true transformation.

Bite Sized Approach

I had to be honest with myself to break the cycle of being on autopilot, no matter how hard that was. I was already working on growing inside—my relationship with God was getting stronger, my faith was being restored, and having hope was encouraging me to dare to dream again. It was time for me to take those small changes I had already made and expand upon them.

The thought of doing anything out of my normal routine scared me, but I knew something had to change. The first thing I did was set a timer for fifteen minutes as I picked up my planner to clean it out. I wanted to remove everything that was past due or outdated so I could put in what was current. This small change meant I wouldn't be faced with regret every time I opened the planner when I saw blank pages from months prior that I hadn't filled out. I knew that when the timer went off, I had to stop the task, so I made sure to make every minute count.

The next thing I did was reset the timer, and I began to plan out the next three months. I knew I needed some time to think through what I was planning and realistically fifteen minutes wouldn't be enough time, but I also knew that in setting the timer, I had to make every minute count, so I worked as quickly as I could. When the timer went off, I wasn't finished, but I had more time I could put into the task, so I reset the timer for another fifteen minutes.

The point of doing it this way was to work on something different in short bursts so that it didn't feel overwhelming. I went into each task with only one expectation—work on that one task the full time and when the timer went off, stop what I was doing and be ok with what progress I made. Because I also like competition, I thrived under the pressure of the short time limit to complete a task, and it gave me something to look forward to conquering.

I challenged myself to do this fifteen minute exercise every day, at least once a day, on projects that felt daunting. I made a to-do list of projects that ranged in size that I had been putting off. Little by little, fifteen minutes by fifteen minutes, I chipped away at things that I had left to the wayside until one by one, I was able to fully mark them off my to-do list. This bite sized approach was easier to attain and achieve than forcing myself to work on one big project from beginning to end. My house may not yet be fully back on track, but it is getting there thanks to making the most of every single fifteen minute timer I could.

You Can Survive the Hardest Days

When it comes to living on autopilot, our tasks aren't the only area where we may find things that have suffered. Chances are if you are on autopilot, your relationships are suffering as well—both externally and internally. Once I became aware of my lack of drive, I began looking into all areas of my life and was met with a reality that frightened me. I had to get real honest with God and with my spouse before I could fully begin to work my way out of it.

One thing that we have to accept is that we can't control the timeline it would take to fully recover from the way we have been living to start living the way we want to be living. It will take hard work and discipline to recreate new habits that are healthier and more loving—to yourself and others. There will be days you want to give up and go back to how things were because it was easier on autopilot, but those are the days to push yourself to break the patterns of destruction that may have entered your life.

When we are at our lowest, those are the days we don't have the energy to get up out of bed and wash our hair, let alone set a fifteen minute timer to work on a task that feels impossible. I have those days, where my mind wrestles with my heart. For those days, I have established my self-care is an essential routine. If I wake up and feel like I just can't even, I make sure I shower first and follow up with a fifteen minute light impact yoga stretching session, and devotionals with a prayer to center myself. If as the day progresses, it gets harder, I take a break in the afternoon where I indulge in putting on one of my favorite face masks that help tone and tighten my skin while playing my favorite music to lift my spirits.

By learning to recognize what it takes to help myself survive the hardest days, I can start reducing the number of hard days by taking ownership of my actions and how they contribute to my emotions. You have all that you need already to do the same. All you have to do is get started, little by little, fifteen minutes by fifteen minutes.

Identity Struggle

Being stuck on autopilot can make us unrecognizable even to ourselves the moment we go from living the same routine daily to suddenly changing it up. The realities we avoided facing will come to the surface which makes it difficult to see the light at the end of the tunnel. Pray for God to give you the strength to start living your life to its fullest again. Extend yourself grace as you try each day to get farther and farther, reawakening your faith as you go.

If we remain on autopilot, waiting for a sign to come while not taking action, we may find that we miss out on the amazing things God has in store for us. The risk of autopilot is not being able to get back the time lost as each day quickly ends. The continuation of these patterns makes it harder and harder to initiate a change that breaks the cycle, but with God's help, you will be able to do so.

How many times do we say, I'll get to that tomorrow, only to let tomorrow pass us by?

Glimpses of Grace

When it comes to living on autopilot, one passage that helped me understand the severity of my situation was the third chapter of Revelation. Jesus addresses the church in Laodicea, which had become lukewarm in its faith—neither hot nor cold. I know that when I live on autopilot, I, too, am lukewarm in my faith. Breaking free from this pattern helps us to more clearly see the direction and purpose God has before us to uncover who we are authentically in Him. Let's read together:

> To the angel of the church in Laodicea write: These are the words of the Amen, the faithful and true witness, the ruler of God's creation. I know your deeds, that you are neither cold nor hot. I wish you were either one or the other! So, because you are lukewarm—neither hot nor cold—I am about to spit you out of my mouth.—Revelation 3:14–16

Grace is found in the call to repentance by Jesus to the Church through his counsel to change. Much like the Church, Jesus asks us to repent and change our ways of complacency. He doesn't want us to be living a lukewarm life, He wants us to live a life that is warm and thriving with Him at the forefront.

> You say, 'I am rich; I have acquired wealth and do not need a thing.' But you do not realize that you are wretched, pitiful, poor, blind and

naked. I counsel you to buy from me gold refined in the fire, so you can become rich; and white clothes to wear, so you can cover your shameful nakedness; and salve to put on your eyes, so you can see.—Revelation 3:17–18

Grace is found in the offerings presented by Jesus. The gold Jesus offers represents the refining grace of God that transforms and purifies us. The white clothes Jesus offers symbolize the purity that comes through God's grace by covering our sinfulness. The salve for the eyes suggests spiritual insight or understanding that comes through God's grace, allowing us to see ourselves and our condition more clearly. By accepting the gifts He offers us, we can be transformed, made pure, and will begin to see more clearly the plan God has in place for us.

The Heart of the Matter: Reawakening Your Faith

The moment you discover you're living in this state it is time to reawaken your faith to go from autopilot to Christ-centered living. You cannot get out of autopilot without God helping you out of it.

It was when I discovered that I was running on autopilot that I learned the importance of time blocking, task lists, timers, and goals. I shifted my morning time block to allow more time for prayer and bible study while drinking coffee or eating breakfast. I made a goal to do this daily for a month, then daily for six months, and then daily for a year.

At first, I didn't think I would survive past a month, but as I celebrated my one year mark of daily devotions and prayer, I thanked God for the strength and His company through it all. Realizing I could maintain a consistent schedule helped me break autopilot and start living each day more intentionally and more Christ-centered.

What is one area in your life that you can take control of again and start scheduling in a way that honors God? Is there a task that you can do right now for fifteen minutes that would help get you back on track and reawaken your faith in the process? I encourage you to do all that you can to break free from the grasp of being on autopilot and start living a more intentional life.

Finding Joy

God can pilot us out of autopilot when we put Him first. By choosing to make time to deepen our faith daily, God shows up and directs us down the path He has intended for us. Letting Him pilot us gives room for spiritual growth and a deeper connection with Him.

By breaking free from a life on autopilot, I am now able to see life in a whole new light—one that I thought I'd never see again. As a result of this, I am also consistently happier, less stressed, and everything I do is filled with purpose and intent. This helps open our eyes to see that life has a meaning, which I'll share with you in the next chapter.

When anxiety leaves your body, there is more room for joy to fill its place. Try not to let the feeling of being overwhelmed by the state things are in keep you from taking the first step, give yourself grace and try again. Joy is found in taking necessary action to reclaim your life again.

Anchor Points

Rediscovering your authentic self and rebuilding your faith takes time. Be patient with yourself and trust that God will guide you through these exercises. Each one is meant to be an anchor point to help keep you authentically anchored in Christ.

Affirm

Write the following scripture somewhere you will see it daily. Memorize it, and refer to it when you lose faith in who you are.

"Teach us to number our days, that we may gain a heart of wisdom."
—Psalm 90:12

Prayer

Heavenly Father, thank you for helping me recognize the importance of living a life filled with intent and purpose alongside of you. I pray, Lord, and ask that you help me to see my life through your eyes, help me to know when I am living on autopilot, and help me to trust you to bring me through it. I pray, Lord, for strength as I face each new day, and the courage to take action fifteen minutes at a time. Thank you, Lord, for being my pilot and helping me to see life in a whole new light, Amen.

Journal Prompt

As I look around my house, I see reflections of the state my mind is in and what I am seeing is…

_____

_____

_____

_____

_____

_____

_____

_____

_____

_____

Declaration Statements

"I am" statement: Write a statement about who you feel you are in this very moment. *Example: I am exhausted.*

I am

_____

_____

"I hope to be" statement: Write a statement about who you hope to be by the end of this book. *Example: I hope to be a good steward of my time and home.*

I hope to be

_____

_____

Chapter Nine
Life Has a Meaning

In my early twenties, I was a leader in youth ministry. I felt it was an honor being placed on my heart by God, and I did everything I could to help where I could. I couldn't help but be saddened by the fact that I knew I wasn't fulfilling my call to serve to its fullest. I was content in youth ministry, and I didn't want to disappoint anyone by telling them I felt as though I was being called to do more when I wasn't quite sure what the call was for.

I attended a women's conference with a group of women from my church that fired me up for the Lord. With every person who spoke, I felt as if God was speaking directly to me. I wrote notes down as fast as I could, desperate to not lose any of it. We broke for lunch and sat in the fellowship hall eating our boxed lunches with turkey sandwiches on croissants. As I took another bite, I remember first thinking, *this is the best sandwich I've ever tasted,* followed by, *I think I'm supposed to be doing more than what I'm doing.* I let my mind wander on that last thought about what more I could potentially be doing and opened myself to daydream about leading a retreat for women of all ages and what that could look like.

Lost in thought, the pastor's wife asked me why I was so quiet and what I was in deep thought about. I could feel the heat rise on my face as my cheeks undoubtedly turned scarlet because I was embarrassed about my inner mulling of being a ministry leader. I laughed nervously and said, "This sandwich is literally the best I've ever had," and joined in their conversations while burying this call into ministry seed in the back of my mind. The fear of rejection and humiliation caused me to silence the call to service I felt in my heart that day, assuming they would think I was ill-equipped.

As the years passed, life events seemed to reinforce my burying the call placed on my heart that day. For years, I kept the seed tucked safely away in the back of my mind where it couldn't be watered. I did continue in youth ministry for the next five years. Shortly after my divorce, I volunteered at Church for a short time and continued to help wherever I was needed until judgment seeped in and I was told I could no longer serve due to my past. I remember the disappointment I had as I packed up my belongings and left the Church that morning, never to return. I picked up a new label that read *rejected*, as I added it onto the anchor chain and kept moving forward.

Twelve years later, when I was stuck in my bottom of the ocean season, life as I had known it was completely different for me. I lost nearly all the support I had, including that of the Church and other friends of faith. It seemed they were choosing to separate themselves from me due to the negativity that came because of the grief I was experiencing. This came as a shock as I had devoted my life to serving God in ministry and walked in faith consistently, and when those whom I considered to be close friends with genuine connections told me they could no longer be my friend, my faith began to slip further and further away. The reality is, I felt abandoned by the Church, by my friends, and by God. When I needed a beacon of light the most, I was met with more darkness.

Because of the hurt I experienced; I allowed myself to throw walls up so high that even I couldn't see over them. In doing so, I became numb and disconnected as I searched for purpose and direction. There was a moment when the call to serve resurfaced in a memory, and I found myself laughing off the notion, pushing that urging further into the shadows, determined to keep it buried for as long as possible. The thought of heeding that call seemed absurd; my past attempts at service had faltered, leading me to reject the invitation to serve once more.

To this day, it saddens me when I think of the precious time I lost because I was afraid to let people in, afraid to take risks and dare to dream, and afraid to do anything that would require me to feel any emotion that could potentially lead to heartache again. Yet at the same time, it also brings me joy knowing that I endured all that I did so I could become a beacon of light to someone hurting alone in the darkness…*you.*

Planting Seeds

During my Monday video chats in 2020, I returned to creative writing. Working on my fiction novel became a gateway for confessing long-hidden desires, aspirations I had shelved in favor of letting my fictional characters live them out on my behalf. This revival in my passion for writing coincided perfectly with Mike's newfound interest in camping, offering me a fresh perspective and a novel outlet for exploration, both on the page and in the wilderness.

We had discussed this before, shortly after the Cherokee trip, and had been preparing to purchase a small couple's trailer to go camping in but had been delayed in the process. I was hesitant, I'll admit. I'm not someone who generally enjoys camping, and I despise bugs. I prefer beach condos for vacationing with a big fluffy bed and a balcony that overlooks the beach whenever possible. But, I was also eager to deepen my connection with him by doing things he enjoyed, and as we packed up our new RV a year later to go camping, I felt both nervous and excited.

Imagine my surprise when on our first trip, the peace that silence offered hooked on camping and reminded me of the power of God's beauty outdoors. I quickly fell into a morning routine where I took my coffee, devotions, and laptop outside to watch the sun come up and spent that time recording everything that came to mind in silence. Mike and I would take afternoon walks, and we began to dream a bit bigger as we discussed the 'what ifs' and 'what's next' moments.

Allowing myself to get lost in nature more frequently forced me to unplug from work and be more present. It wasn't long before God began to meet me with a reminder of the seed I had buried, by gently surfacing it from hiding. As a result, I began looking forward to camping so I could spend my mornings in silence in hopes of uncovering directions that came from prayers with God. Yet, hindered by self-doubt and reluctance to embrace my calling, I found God's voice remained silent, and the seed weakened, untended and unwatered.

What did happen, however, was Mike and I began to form a deeper connection and I could see glimpses of joy returning to both of us as we would laugh at ourselves while we fumbled with trying to put together a camping chair we bought for the dog so we could keep her off of ours. We started sitting around the campsite every evening where we would engage in discussions, about anything and everything we could think of.

On one trip as I was writing, I glanced up to see he had fallen asleep; the sun glistened on the water just beyond him. I found myself staring at him, remembering all the wonderful things we had done together, and I gave thanks to God for all of it, for bringing Mike into my life so I would have someone to grow old with. I began praying that if ministry was something God was calling me to, He would equip and prepare both of us to be able to handle it together because life with him was so precious, and I wanted to enjoy every moment with him by my side.

Trusting God

Over time, God began opening new doors for me within my design business. As a result, I found myself falling back into familiar patterns of busy-ness. In doing so, I began to recognize my unhappiness as I was spending all my time working, and not enough time on the things that made me happy. I questioned what the purpose of hustling like this was. Did my life have a meaning that went beyond working all the time or was this it for me? I feared I would settle back into a life on autopilot after having worked so hard to get out of it.

As I sat down to write a chapter in the novel I was working on, a fictional romance book I had been writing for almost a year, my progress was thrown off as I began typing out what was on my heart instead. I read back my confessions through tears running down my face, only to realize, *she* (my fictional character) was telling *my* story and not her own. My tears didn't just get wiped away and discarded, they became the water to the buried seed God had replanted that day at the camper. This water provided the valuable nutrients for God's call to sprout at last. It was then when I realized the first step in answering the call to serve was to step out on faith, trusting God fully to help me do the unthinkable— to share my story of identity crisis and how God was bringing me to a place of finally knowing who I am.

People have asked me lately how I knew God was calling me to tell my story. They wanted to know if I heard Him audibly speak it into existence or if it was more of an inner knowing. The answer to that is no, there was no loud booming voice, no bright light, no angel standing before me. There was only a confession of my heart staring back at me on the computer screen, accompanied by peace and understanding that this is what I'm being asked to do. I have lived a lifetime of running and hiding from my truth to keep the skeletons of my past buried deep in the closet of shame. This was a big ask of God on me, yet I rejoiced in being chosen to teach His word alongside my story. I stopped running, and on this day I simply said yes.

What I wasn't prepared for was where I am today as I write this chapter. God has already revealed to me in all the chapters leading up to this one exactly what it is He is calling me to do, which I never thought would be possible. That seed is no longer a sprout, it's rapidly growing before my very eyes as it points the way to the ministry He has been calling me to since my early twenties.

Friend, God has a purpose for you, your life does have meaning. Chances are you've known it for a long time, but because life has been so difficult, it feels like it was just a dream. Meet God where it is quiet, allow Him the chance to firmly plant that seed within you, and give Him the space to work within you so that the seed can be watered and begin to grow.

Identity Struggle

We often feel like we aren't qualified to do things we are called to do, especially when we've never done them before. It's natural to have this same sensation when we feel God is moving us to do something bigger than we are. When I first had the thought of starting a women's ministry in my twenties, I hid from that call by focusing on the fear of rejection and humiliation that I believed would happen. That day at the conference, I didn't even give the women a chance to support me or pray with me because of my fear.

I've always been a firm believer that everything happens in God's perfect timing, and my situation is no different in that I know that now is a time when it is right for me to step out in faith and start the ministry God is calling me to. Had I decided in my twenties to do the same, I likely would have failed because the timing wasn't right. God has been equipping me through the lessons learned over the last twenty-five years, using these lessons as stepping stones in helping others who are experiencing similar trials as what I have journeyed.

He has lovingly put women in my path who need to hear my story of resiliency that brought me to where I am today so that they can hope that they, too, can get through whatever darkness they are currently facing. Time is never wasted; it is in the times we struggle that we can look back and see that God lovingly helped us get through and that our pain has a purpose. Your life's story qualifies you to serve God in the way He is calling you to. You have what it takes, you are enough.

My question for you is: how has your journey prepared you to answer God's call, even when you feel inadequate? Your life is beautifully ordained by God in a way that your light shines so brightly that others can see their way out of darkness through you.

Glimpses of Grace

There is one person who comes to mind when I think about someone who courageously answers the call to step out in faith and make a bold statement—Esther. The book of Esther recounts her story in its entirety, which I recommend you take time to read in full. Today, I will focus on a few passages so we can see where grace was found in her calling and how it can be applied to us in ours. Let's take a look at the text beginning in Esther chapter 4:

> *When Esther's words were reported to Mordecai, he sent back this answer: 'Do not think that because you are in the king's house you alone of all the Jews will escape. For if you remain silent at this time,*

relief and deliverance for the Jews will arise from another place, but
you and your father's family will perish. And who knows but that you
have come to your royal position for such a time as this?' Then Esther
sent this reply to Mordecai: 'Go, gather together all the Jews who are
in Susa, and fast for me. Do not eat or drink for three days, night or
day. I and my attendants will fast as you do. When this is done, I will
go to the king, even though it is against the law. And if I perish, I
*perish.' —*Esther 4:12–16

Grace is found in Esther's courage to answer the call to speak on behalf of the Jews, risking her life in her quest to aid in the deliverance of the Jews. Esther's purpose as Queen was what led her to this very moment. Though she felt inadequate to speak to the King, she took time to prepare for what was to come, even if it was death. Much like Esther's courage, you also have courage within you to live a purpose-filled life as ordained by God despite the challenging situations you have faced. He will prepare you with all that you need to answer and fulfill His calling.

Esther again pleaded with the king, falling at his feet and weeping.
She begged him to put an end to the evil plan of Haman the Agagite,
which he had devised against the Jews. Then the king extended the
gold scepter to Esther and she arose and stood before him. 'If it pleases
the king,' she said, 'and if he regards me with favor and thinks it
the right thing to do, and if he is pleased with me, let an order be
written overruling the dispatches that Haman son of Hammedatha,
the Agagite, devised and wrote to destroy the Jews in all the king's
provinces. For how can I bear to see disaster fall on my people? How
*can I bear to see the destruction of my family?' —*Esther 8:3–6

Grace is found when the King listens to Esther and again when he mercifully extends the gold scepter to her. Grace is also found in God's plan coming to fruition through the courage of Esther to answer her call to go forth. Much like God's plan for Esther, He also has a plan and purpose set for you. It is up to you to seek out direction to uncover exactly what that is.

The Heart of the Matter: Answering Your Call

As I am going through the editing process of my book, I have a confession to make: When I wrote this chapter four months ago, I was certain that a women's ministry is what I was called to do, but the more I would explore and plan out the details surrounding the ministry, I would run into a brick wall at full force. Something still felt off, not quite right. It was missing the potential to reach a younger generation, where my call into ministry first began. The more I planned, the more I began to question: *What about the children?*

When it comes to answering the call you feel God is placing on your heart, pray for guidance and direction. If you struggle to determine exactly what it is you should do, there are resources you can find online to gain clarity on the topic before you to aide in decision making. Don't rush into it, preparing to enter a season of ministry takes time to build a solid foundation, and when we rush, important things may get missed.

Whether God is calling you to help a friend, foster a child, or write your story, He will equip you with all that you need, but you must first ask Him.

Finding Joy

My friend, God is calling us to serve Him in some capacity. It could be as simple as designing a brand kit for a small business, or as complex as starting a ministry like in my situation. Dare to say yes when He calls upon you again. Know that not everyone recognizes the calling in the same way. Each of us has a unique relationship with God and it is genuine to you. You'll know it when it's the only thing you can think about for days on end, a constant beacon, everything you see reminds you of it, it is in that moment, that you'll know. I pray you'll have the courage to say yes and welcome change with open arms. We'll talk about how hard change can be in the next chapter. Joy is found the moment you surrender to God and say yes to whatever it is He is calling you to do.

Anchor Points

Rediscovering your authentic self and rebuilding your faith takes time. Be patient with yourself and trust that God will guide you through these exercises. Each one is meant to be an anchor point to help keep you authentically anchored in Christ.

Affirm

Write the following scripture somewhere you will see it daily. Memorize it, and refer to it when you lose faith in who you are.

"'I am the Lord's servant,' Mary answered. May your word to me be fulfilled." —Luke 1:38

Prayer

Heavenly Father, thank you for believing in me even with all that I have gone through. Lord, I know you have been calling me to do something, but I often let fear win and dismiss the thought before it has the chance to take root. Lord, I ask that you please make known to me your purpose and plan for my life, help me to see and know the signs you place before me. Thank you, Lord, for choosing me to help others find their way to your kingdom, Amen.

Journal Prompt

Looking back at everything I have gone through; I feel my lessons are...

_____
_____
_____
_____
_____
_____
_____
_____
_____
_____
_____
_____
_____
_____
_____
_____
_____
_____
_____
_____
_____
_____
_____

Declaration Statements

"I am" statement: Write a statement about who you feel you are in this very moment. *Example: I am chosen.*

I am

_____

_____

"I hope to be" statement: Write a statement about who you hope to be by the end of this book. *Example: I hope to be a beacon of light for others in need.*

I hope to be

_____

_____

chapter Ten
Change is Hard

I am someone who has gotten to the point of liking predictability and am not a fan of surprises no matter how good they claim to be. To me, predictability meant safety, which was something I needed to be at peace. I am perfectly content living my life in a way that doesn't put a giant spotlight on me and will even go so far as to allow others to take recognition for my hard work. For the longest time, I have said that I am the best kept secret in graphic design among my peers. Not many people knew that I could even design, let alone that I did it for a living, and I was okay with that in the beginning. However, as I got to the point of wanting to scale my business, I knew that I would have to change my presentation.

Begrudgingly, I decided to become more active on social media by sharing bits of wisdom I had when it came to running a small business. The more I put myself out for the public to see, the more I was met with criticism. I found that the internet was full of people who were quick to tear me down on my weight, appearance, and clothing. This became exhausting and caused me to lose belief in my skills and capabilities, even though I knew I was good at my work.

I envied people who seemed to take harsh judgments from others and carried on as if it didn't bother them. That was not something I could do because of my emotions. I had always been labeled as being overly sensitive, and as I've aged, I have come to embrace my empathy as a rare quality that not many people have or understand.

I have struggled to feel understood and have often complained that others simply didn't listen to me. However, I've come to realize perhaps it was not that they weren't listening but that they couldn't fully understand my unique blend of empathy combined with logic. I was unable to effectively communicate with those different from me. I knew I couldn't change this emotional part of me because it is something God has instilled in me as a gift to use in a way that others cannot, but what I could change was my approach to communication.

During a discussion on web design, a peer offhandedly remarked that as a graphic designer, I couldn't possibly excel in web design too. They seemed convinced that my expertise was confined to a single discipline, unaware of my years of experience in designing websites. This attempt to pigeonhole me felt like an effort to question my qualifications. Typically, such skepticism might have riled me up, prompting an emotional defense of my skills. But this time, I simply smiled and gently corrected them, sharing insights into my multifaceted work portfolio that spoke volumes about my capabilities.

Despite having been able to successfully change how I reacted to a stressful conversation, it still hurt me emotionally after the conversation ended. One thing I had only admitted to my closest friends was my feeling of inadequacy despite being trained in design. My poor self-esteem was something I carried with me from childhood. It started back on that playground where the kids seemingly did everything they could to make me cry while they laughed. Therefore, low self-esteem was something I wrestled with daily and something that threatened to stop me from fulfilling my dreams. Life and the way others treated me caused me to feel broken and unworthy.

You can see why saying no to leading a women's ministry was so easy for me. After all, I didn't believe that I had what it took to do the job because I had lost sight of the big picture: I am worth more than many sparrows.

Are not two sparrows sold for a penny? Yet not one of them will fall to the ground outside your Father's care. And even the very hairs of your head are all numbered. So don't be afraid; you are worth more than many sparrows.—Matthew 10:29–31

God cares and values you, if He cares for even the smallest of creatures like sparrows, then surely He cares for you, His child. Do not be afraid, but trust in God for His provisions and love.

Overcoming Analysis Paralysis

Change comes in many forms, it's not always just in changing the way you approach conversations, it could be changing your appearance, or even changing your job. I had gotten to the point where change frightened me so much that it would cause anxiety within me, leaving my soul in a constant state of unrest and worry. I would torture myself by over-analyzing everything and when it came to making decisions, I would have analysis paralysis so bad that I would shut down emotionally.

I wasn't always this indecisive. Before losing the kids, I made decisions confidently and quickly that were always relatively good and often had good outcomes. Somehow having control over a situation removed *from* me while decisions were made *for* me caused me to question everything I decided on. Suddenly, the simple question 'What's for dinner' felt like the equivalent of deciding something that would drastically change the course of my life even though it was merely a choice of salad or nachos.

I no longer trusted that I had good judgment or decision-making skills because the last big decision that was made resulted in heartbreak. I knew that to get back to a place of confidence I would need to rely on God's help because this indecisiveness and low self-esteem had a tight grip on me. I also knew that the reason this had gotten to this point was due to believing a mountain of limiting beliefs about myself because I gave weight to the remarks others had made to me.

I remembered an exercise a friend suggested I do, which involved a mirror and a dry erase marker, so I grabbed a dry erase marker and headed to my bathroom where I could get started. I stood staring at myself for quite some time as I thought of all the limiting beliefs that were needing to be conquered first. I was too afraid to admit to some of them, but I knew to move forward I had to do this. Using the dry erase marker, I wrote the opposite of what I believed to be true on the mirror around my head. The point of the exercise is to leave the words there until you believe them to be true, and then you erase them and replace them with others that may come up.

The first three I picked were (uneducated) experienced, (not good enough) qualified, (fat) healthy. I stopped after that last one and rolled my eyes at myself. One would likely be up for all of eternity because being called fat has happened to me since childhood, and believing I was healthy despite knowing I was trying to be would be difficult. I continued with adding words one by one until I started running out of room, only two more words would fit, so I ended with (broken) unbroken, and (insufficient) enough.

I stepped back and looked at my words, understanding that as I read each one, I was living a life in the opposites. To break the cycle of being forever stuck in analysis paralysis, I would have to start believing those words were true so I could start living them daily. I made it a goal to work on one word a week starting with experienced. I sought out training on basic web coding to better understand how to make changes within the structure of the website to match the design that I wanted. The more I learned, the more I began to believe in my experience as a designer, and so I removed the word.

Acceptance of Change

It is in doing the very things we believe we can't do that we prove to ourselves we can. I also adopted a philosophy that I was no longer in competition with anyone but who I was yesterday as I strive to be better today. Each person is on their journey, bringing with them skills and experiences that are unique to them. I knew that if I wanted to embrace my authentic self for who I was to my core, I would have to start learning to discover what was beneath the surface that I was still hiding even from myself. It was also crucial for me to not compare myself or my progress to that of anyone else, because in doing so, it would threaten my ability to change from this imposter I had allowed to surface in place of the person I hid below.

As you set out to change the person you have become due to surviving the hurt you endured, it will cause you to be vulnerable and real with yourself. It's not every day you wake up and look in the mirror and see words that describe a person you once were that somehow along the way you've drifted far away from. I must confess that I got mad at myself often on my quest to change, so much so that I erased all the words from my mirror out of frustration. I had to ask myself if I was sabotaging my progress out of fear of becoming a version of me that I knew could never be fully put back together properly, to which I already knew the answer.

The truth is, friend, you will never be the same. It is impossible to be that version of you that you are longing to be again. The person you are right now has traveled through some pretty rocky roads to reach where you are today. You have adapted and grown, learning valuable lessons you will carry with you as you desperately seek to discover who you are in this new season of life. With God's help, you will become the woman He created you to be, using each stone as a piece of the puzzle that unveils a beautiful destination that has been waiting for you all along.

God has been calling me to step out in faith since my twenties to lead a ministry, but I have denied the call every step of the way. I have lacked confidence because I felt ill-equipped to serve, but I know that I must change this misbelief by learning everything I can on the subject, and so I pour myself into research, reading His word, prayer, and constant communication with God. Simply putting one foot in front of the next in simple obedience to my Heavenly Father—He equips us with what we need to fulfill His call.

As I look behind me at the rubble in my road, I can see how each piece can be used to build upon each other, fitting in perfectly to create the most magnificent place for others to gather in fellowship. It is in seeing this vision that I can now confidently say a resounding yes to God as I begin to put into motion plans to open a ministry in the coming years.

What change is before you now? If you were to write down the opposite of all the misbeliefs you have about yourself, would you be overwhelmed or full of hope?

Change is hard but have faith that God will see you through it. *"Blessed is the one who perseveres under trial because, having stood the test, that person will receive the crown of life that the Lord has promised to those who love him"* (James 1:12).

Identity Struggle

My identity struggle was the worst when faced with the thought of changing who I was. I had a hard time determining who I wanted to be because I couldn't recognize who I had become. The one thing I remembered was before my bottom of the ocean moment, there was joy and purpose in my life, and I longed to have that again. The reality was, I knew I could never be the same as I once was, because life lessons had molded me into this new person that I wasn't proud of becoming.

Once I was able to discover the negative qualities I had picked up and held onto, I was then able to see how changing them to positive again could help bring me to a place that I was proud of. Even though I turned my back on God, I had never forgotten His love for me. I struggled with accepting that I was forgiven for my sins and loved in my entirety because I felt flawed, and because so many times I had been rejected.

By looking behind me at the road I've traveled with a fresh perspective, I no longer saw the rocky terrain as obstacles, instead, God showed me the possibilities I could create by using the ruins to rebuild.

How many times do you focus on negativity because it feels like the only emotion you feel, instead of trusting God as He shows you the positive that is in your journey?

Glimpses of Grace

When it comes to stepping into our calling and making changes within ourselves to be prepared to answer, there is one story in the Bible that shows us a struggle like what we face today. The calling of Gideon comes to mind. In Judges chapter 6 we read the story of Gideon and how he was called by God to lead the Israelites in a time of great adversity. At first, Gideon was hesitant and unsure of himself, but through a series of signs and encouragement from God, he embraced his role and led the

Israelites to victory over their oppressors. This story gives me hope that I, too, can have victory over those who continually cast judgment on me with the help of the Lord. Let's read together:

The angel of the Lord came and sat down under the oak in Ophrah that belonged to Joash the Abiezrite, where his son Gideon was threshing wheat in a winepress to keep it from the Midianites. When the angel of the Lord appeared to Gideon, he said, 'The Lord is with you, mighty warrior.' 'Pardon me, my lord,' Gideon replied, 'but if the Lord is with us, why has all this happened to us? Where are all his wonders that our ancestors told us about when they said, "Did not the Lord bring us up out of Egypt?" But now the Lord has abandoned us and given us into the hand of Midian.' The Lord turned to him and said, 'Go in the strength you have and save Israel out of Midian's hand. Am I not sending you?' 'Pardon me, my lord,' Gideon replied, 'but how can I save Israel? My clan is the weakest in Manasseh, and I am the least in my family.' The Lord answered, 'I will be with you, and you will strike down all the Midianites, leaving none alive.' — Judges 6:11–16*

Grace is found in Gideon, where he admits that he has doubts that God is with them, especially with the difficulties they are facing. Much like Gideon, we often doubt God's presence with us during our hardest times. It's not that we don't love God, it's that we are so blinded by our hurt that we can't see God through our tears. Grace is also found in God's call and assurance that He will be with Gideon as he carries out his calling. God will go with us wherever He calls us to go. God wants us to be successful in our calling, so He will equip us with all that we need to be able to achieve greatness for His kingdom.

Gideon replied, 'If now I have found favor in your eyes, give me a sign that it is really you talking to me. Please do not go away until I come back and bring my offering and set it before you.' And the Lord said, 'I will wait until you return.' —Judges 6:17–18*

Grace is found when God agrees to wait until Gideon returns despite his disbelief in Him. Much like Gideon, God also waits patiently and loving on us until we return to Him, wholly and authentically ourselves.

The Heart of the Matter: Accept Change as a Path to Growth

When we are faced with a desire to change who we are to become the best authentic versions of ourselves, disbelief comes when what we know to be true turns out to be false. When we try to plan our future without God directing the plan, it becomes twisted along the way. Every time we take one step forward on our own, something happens to cause us to stumble three steps backward.

Don't let your future be defined by your past hardships, part of being able to progress forward means breaking the chains to the anchor that keeps you at the bottom of the ocean. Change is a path to growth, and while it is difficult to accept because it makes us uncomfortable. We are called to act and embrace the change God is guiding us through as we seek His direction in our plans.

Finding Joy

Don't be afraid of change. God knows the path that lies before us as He has already painted the bigger picture using the path behind us. We need to trust Him in this season of uncertainty as we push ourselves out of our comfort zones so we can start living life to the fullest again.

Take the labels of misbelief and turn them into qualities that fill your life with joy and purpose. You have the power within you to create a change in your life that is so powerful others will undoubtedly take notice.

Discovering your authentic self is getting closer and closer, you've already come so far to turn back now. Progress can be found in the most surprising of places, and in the next chapter, I'll share with you how paint chips opened my eyes in a whole new way. Joy is found when you change the labels of misbelief into authentic qualities.

Anchor Points

Rediscovering your authentic self and rebuilding your faith takes time. Be patient with yourself and trust that God will guide you through these exercises. Each one is meant to be an anchor point to help keep you authentically anchored in Christ.

Affirm

Write the following scripture somewhere you will see it daily. Memorize it, and refer to it when you lose faith in who you are.

"Commit to the Lord whatever you do and he will establish your plans." —Proverbs 16:3

Prayer

Heavenly Father, thank you for the hard lessons you've brought me through and the reminder that you were with me through it all. Lord, I know I haven't been true to myself or you. I ask that you help me uncover the negativities in my life that need to be transformed into positivities. Please give me the strength to face each of these areas head on so I can begin to conquer them one by one as I start to move forward again. Thank you, Lord, for waiting patiently on me, Amen.

Journal Prompt

One area that I have become most negative and need to change is...

_____

_____

_____

_____

_____

_____

_____

_____

_____

_____

_____

_____

_____

_____

_____

_____

_____

_____

_____

_____

_____

_____

_____

_____

Declaration Statements

"I am" statement: Write a statement about who you feel you are in this very moment. *Example: I am qualified.*

I am

_____

_____

"I hope to be" statement: Write a statement about who you hope to be by the end of this book. *Example: I hope to be a good leader for God's kingdom.*

I hope to be

_____

_____

Chapter Eleven
Paint Chips = Progress

When I discovered I was living on autopilot, I sat in our living room looking around at everything and realizing that nothing had changed since we moved in. Sure, there were a few new pieces, but for the most part, it was the same as it had always been. I didn't love the colors on our walls. They were colors that had been here when we moved in, and due to lack of time and not knowing what we wanted to paint the walls back then, we opted to match the paint left behind and give it all a quick fresh coat with the thought that we'd refresh it when it needed it.

After we had been selected for foster placement, the timing wasn't right to paint, and the walls took a beating with the rambunctious children who inhabited the space, which only further delayed the process on the main floor. Upstairs, the kids each had their bedrooms, where we allowed them to help in the decision making and painted their rooms according to each of their colorful tastes. Against my better judgment, I painted murals on their focal walls, each of them tied in their overall theme.

After two years of building a family with them, they moved out. I simply closed both bedroom doors and left everything as it was when they left. There were many times I would sneak off into the closed rooms and sit on the floor and cry, wishing I could hug them both again, praying that God would keep them safe. This went on for another year until there was a need to convert one of the rooms into Mike's home office.

When the time came to repaint, my heart ached at the thought of altering the rooms that were meant for them, fearing the day might come when I'd have to explain why their spaces had changed. Deep down, I understood the slim chances of their return, and the necessity of moving forward. We chose a dark gunmetal gray, a color given to us, to cover the walls. The process of erasing the mural was emotionally taxing; tears fell as we silently worked, painting over our once vibrant hopes and dreams, sealing them beneath the new hue in just a few hours.

I knew we needed to do the same in the second bedroom, but the emotional toil of changing one was enough to delay progress on the second room for four years. I simply wasn't ready to fully let go of the remaining indication that there once were children in this home that I cared for deeply. I did, however, agree to purge the remaining items we had purchased in preparation for foster care and boxed up everything I was ready to part with.

Eventually we repainted the second bedroom in a neutral tan color so I could have a place to manufacture my notepads and take product photography. I felt that for me to be okay with erasing what once was in that room, I had to make it one that I could use consistently. Because some time had passed from the first room to the second, I didn't cry as I painted it. Instead, I smiled at the memories as I covered them up, forever etching in my brain what that room once looked like.

That was as far as I could go. Even though I was okay with the result of both rooms, I still felt like I was betraying them somehow by covering up something familiar to them. There was no way I was ready to repaint the main floor, despite it desperately needing it.

Before I knew it, more precious time had slipped by. In total, eight years had now passed since our children had left, and I suddenly found myself increasingly disturbed by the state of our walls. They seemed to echo back to me the years of autopilot I had lived through, demanding a change I could no longer ignore. It consumed my thoughts for weeks until I broached the subject with Mike, suggesting we start with just the dining room as a test, to see if we were ready for the transformation.

We made our way to the paint store where I was immediately overwhelmed. I felt clueless about the exact shade I wanted, so I instinctively reached for colors that resonated with me within the coastal palette, echoing my home's existing decor. However, once surrounded by the countless single swatches I had picked up, a wave of dissatisfaction washed over me. They all felt wrong, and I couldn't quite figure out why. It occurred to me that in my desire to become my more authentic self, my affection for the coastal theme that once defined our home no longer resonated with who I was becoming.

Make Bold Choices

Rebuilding after a crisis looks different for everyone, as each of us is different in who we are. Some people can bounce back much quicker than others, while others may struggle to make simple decisions—like choosing a paint color. I had found myself in another one of those analysis paralysis moments that I had been working so hard to stay out of. The growth I recognized within me at this moment was that the reason for the uncertainty was due to my tastes and style changes, not due to the fear of change.

I thought that I had come to know who I was as a person and what it was that I liked, but because I had not yet put that to the test, I didn't know that some things within me had changed. This was another pivotal moment for me as I went from room to room and looked at every single piece of decor and knick-knacks we had accumulated over the years. Each item told a story or was tied into a place in time that I cherished, like the seashells in a bowl collected from the beach on the day Mike and I got married. I wasn't sure if I was ready to change everything drastically yet, but I also knew that we now enjoyed camping and the mountains in addition to the beach. Perhaps it was time to say goodbye to the coastal after all.

I made a bold decision that day asking Mike if we could do a massive purge and begin living a more simplistic life with less stuff. This idea of stripping back everything and starting over felt like a new beginning we both needed. This one conversation led to many more, which ultimately altered our decision to paint the dining room. We decided to undertake a main floor remodel in several different stages spaced out over time, updating light fixtures that have been on the fritz, removing the broken blinds and replacing them with more natural shades, and of course adding a fresh coat of paint in each of the open areas.

I may have spent a little more time in the planning stage than I care to admit, allowing myself the chance to figure out what it was I liked and adding elements that Mike liked. Together, we picked out new paint chips in a more neutral palette that would help us achieve our desire to go more minimalist. I had my eye set on a couple of main colors I was certain would be chosen, so we purchased peel-and-stick samples to put on the walls so I could see them in our spaces.

When we got home, I walked room to room, adding sample chips in different places and putting the peel-and-stick samples in areas I could see from any area in the room at all different times of day. From this thorough exploration, I managed to narrow down my options to five promising colors, feeling a sense of achievement that was both new and intense. This seemingly minor task represented a significant stride forward, marking the first time I genuinely felt I had made significant progress.

Look at the Bigger Picture

When you work hard on making life changes, you naturally become more aligned with God. You'll notice things will start to happen that you least expect. This is proof that God is, indeed, working in your life. There were plenty of times I wanted to give up and say I'm not doing this but as time progressed and as I did the work on my mindset and in my relationship with God, I was able to come to a place of making real progress in an area I had struggled to make a decision before.

My friend, how many times have you wanted to give up because the task at hand felt too overwhelming to complete? Might I suggest that perhaps you are standing too close to the situation to see it for what it is? Take a step back and ask God to help you see the broader view of the situation you're facing. Ask Him for a fresh perspective of what He is doing in your life right now.

As you do this, you can see victories you may have overlooked. It's important for you to celebrate your wins, no matter how small you think they are, because even the smallest step in the right direction is still proof that picking up paint chips equals progress.

Identity Struggle

I'm notoriously critical of myself, particularly when I sense a lack of progress in my journey to rediscover my authentic self and rebuild my faith. Observing others celebrate their significant achievements often leads me to undervalue my own accomplishments, feeling as though I haven't done anything noteworthy.

Something I have learned is that as you consistently show up each day and give God a chance to work in your life, you are making progress in rebuilding your faith. As you make progress in this area, you are also making progress in rediscovering your authentic self. They go together, hand in hand. You cannot do one without the other, and you can do neither without God.

I ask you: How many times do you get down on yourself when it feels like you aren't making progress, even when God shows you the progress you're making in the seemingly small ways?

Glimpses of Grace

God honors even the smallest and most sincere efforts in our spiritual journey. Sometimes, it requires every bit of strength we possess to take steps toward healing and growing in grace. The story of The Widow's Offering in Mark chapter 12 serves as a powerful testimony to this truth. Let's take a closer look together:

> *Jesus sat down opposite the place where the offerings were put and watched the crowd putting their money into the temple treasury. Many rich people threw in large amounts. But a poor widow came and put in two very small copper coins, worth only a few cents.* — Mark 12:41–42

Grace is found when the widow puts her offering in without hesitation. Much like the widow, when you put in your time and effort towards spiritual growth, it shows that you are willing to give it your all, no matter the cost.

Calling his disciples to him, Jesus said, 'Truly I tell you, this poor widow has put more into the treasury than all the others. They all gave out of their wealth; but she, out of her poverty, put in everything— all she had to live on.'—Mark 12:43–44

Grace is found when Jesus acknowledges that the offering given by the widow cost her everything, yet she still gave willingly. Much like Jesus acknowledges your offering toward your spiritual and physical growth as you rediscover your authentic self.

The Heart of the Matter: Rebuilding After Crisis

The call to change leads to small steps that produce progress, which in turn gets us even closer to rediscovering our authentic selves. As we explored in this chapter, rebuilding after going through a crisis takes a lot out of us mentally, emotionally, and physically. Be encouraged that God recognizes even your smallest offerings as a sacrificial giving to Him and His plans for you.

As I shared, I struggled with the thought of even changing the paint color on the walls for several years, fighting the urge to change out of fear. Over time, and as I drew nearer to God, I stopped viewing this as something to fear and started seeing it as an act of obedience.

Finding Joy

Sometimes progress looks like paint chips sitting in a stack on your dining room table displaying a tapestry of color that brings joy to your heart. It's okay to take smaller steps as you rediscover your authentic self during change, and we'll cover more on this in the next chapter. When life is heavy, it takes a ton out of us to do something as simple as picking paint colors, so if all you did today was pick up a stack of paint chips to someday choose from, then you made progress. Joy is found in celebrating the progress you are making, you have worked so hard to come up out of the ocean and get to where you are today, celebrate!

Anchor Points

Rediscovering your authentic self and rebuilding your faith takes time. Be patient with yourself and trust that God will guide you through these exercises. Each one is meant to be an anchor point to help keep you authentically anchored in Christ.

Affirm

Write the following scripture somewhere you will see it daily. Memorize it, and refer to it when you lose faith in who you are.

> *"So whether you eat or drink or whatever you do, do it all for the glory of God."* —1 Corinthians 10:31

Prayer

> *Heavenly Father, thank you for the reminder that even ordinary everyday activities can be done in a way that brings honor to you. On days when I feel like I haven't done enough, please remind me that even the smallest act I make is enough. Thank you, Lord, for helping me work through change and step out more in faith, Amen.*

Journal Prompt

One way I can see I am making progress is…

_____

_____

_____

_____

_____

Declaration Statements

"I am" statement: Write a statement about who you feel you are in this very moment. *Example: I am making some progress.*

I am

_____

_____

"I hope to be" statement: Write a statement about who you hope to be by the end of this book. *Example: I hope to be more consistent in honoring God in all that I do.*

I hope to be

_____

_____

Chapter Twelve
It's Going to Be Okay

Resiliency is not something I have always had within me; it is something that I had to work at consistently. One of my biggest fears is rejection and humiliation. Yet, I have lived a life filled with both, and it never gets any easier to face. One of the things that I have had to do is remind myself that I have faced the clutch of darkness so tight that it dared to snuff out the life within me. Yet somehow, some way, I have come out on the other side of it and found myself back in the light.

At the heart of it, when difficulties arise, I find myself fleeing. I retreat into solitude, deliberately distancing myself from whatever or whoever has caused me distress. My aversion to conflict runs deep; rather than confront or counter, I choose to withdraw. This behavior, I tell myself, is in adherence to Jesus's teachings and instruction not to resist an evil person and instead turn the other cheek (Matthew 5:39). Yet, if I'm truly honest, I respond this way due to my fear of rejection and humiliation.

Due to my history of being hurt, I've built coping mechanisms to navigate the aftermath, invariably casting blame upon myself regardless of the situation. I find myself replaying events, scrutinizing them for a moment where I might have acted or spoken differently, indulging in fantasies of alternative outcomes that are beyond reach. Recognizing this detrimental habit was a crucial step towards cultivating resilience.

To develop resilience, I needed to embrace the role of an observer. I got better at listening intently, paying close attention, and allowing myself the grace of time before responding. This deliberate pause in my reactions became a foundational step in my journey towards the resilience I sought. I began to pray specifically for those with whom I faced ongoing challenges—those whose mere presence triggered my anxiety. I sought God's guidance earnestly, pleading for wisdom on how to navigate situations that left me feeling diminished, and for the strength to approach these encounters with grace and discernment.

After about a year of this, I began noticing the things that triggered a reactive response within me causing anger to surface. I journaled about these deep inner responses to confrontation I was experiencing such as heart palpitations and panic attacks. I drew a conclusion that my impatience with others was contributing to the increase in anxiety I felt. Reading through my journal entries I began noticing a pattern surrounding the onset of most of my panic attacks and it was in the times when I felt unheard, unappreciated, and disrespected.

Shortly after I came up out of the ocean and was back on shore, I decided to take matters into my own hands and wear bravery like a cloak surrounding me as I dared try again, putting myself back out there on social media. I knew how important having a social media presence was to having a successful business. Therefore, I wanted to become more present on social media and provide my followers with content that could really help them and that they could relate to. So, I began sharing again. It was great at first. I was vulnerable, raw, real, and authentic. Unfortunately, a familiar encounter with skepticism and mockery quickly arrived in the form of a message, causing me to be denied the opportunity to demonstrate my value.

Because I hadn't yet reached the level of growth necessary to withstand the criticism I received, I retreated and hid away once more. I retreated into my safe space where I was surrounded by the comfort of my walls, hidden away from the giants standing before me. As a result, my business suffered, I lost sales, I lost followers, and I lost many connections which I had worked hard to build.

Like you, I also had to go through the steps of determining who I was in this new season of life as I learned to love moments spent in solitude, began to see the beauty in God's design, rediscovered my passions, and pulled myself out of living on autopilot. Each stepping stone placed in front of the next helped me to go from lost in the wilderness to back on the right path with God by my side.

I have shared my experiences of becoming authentically anchored and overcoming those challenging periods of time in my life with those I have connected with along the way—people who were at times life preservers on my way back to shore. Through this journey, those new friends and connections have continually shared that there are many out there who need to hear my story, to learn how I was able to get out of the ocean and back to shore. Yet every time I tried to share my story with others, both in person and online, there was always one person whose meanness outshined all of the good and caused me to stop trying.

I realized I had come face to face with my giant. I allowed their words to carry weight as I began to retreat. My fear of being humiliated caused me to give up on myself and my mission to help others. Discovering this, I knew I had to fight my giant: fear. Because I had been putting in the work towards personal growth, I knew this time I stood a chance.

Slay the Giant

No matter what we set out to do in life, there will always be a giant we have to face to move forward. Once we find ourselves standing face to face with the giant before us, we have a choice—we can turn and run, retreating to safety, or we can stay and fight, conquering the giant that stands in our way.

It's amazing to me how I can help others get where they want to go but have such a hard time mapping out a course for myself. Over the years, I have helped countless people find their brand identity through a series of questions and processes I created to help them uncover what was within them. I have mentored other business owners who felt a giant roadblock standing in their way, unsure how to get around it. I listened to their challenges and helped them map out solutions that worked for them. But when it came to this challenging season in my life and with my own business, I couldn't do the same.

I reflected on what I have learned: When we are fixated on the problem before us, we become blind to the possible solutions. I stopped and took a breath, looking around at my situations and how I was able to help so many but couldn't seem to help myself. It was then I finally recognized the necessity of confronting my fear of rejection and humiliation, employing strategies I'd advise my clients to use. I couldn't let fear keep me from focusing on my business, knowing that its success hinges on my ability to be present online.

The only thing I could think to do was study, learn, and practice. I equipped myself with the tools I needed to be successful, and the only thing left was to become more confident in my abilities. I have always taught my clients that confidence isn't something that just springs up overnight, it builds up over time as we make a conscious effort every time we show up. Just when you think you'll never reach the point of becoming confident, you'll surprise yourself by doing the most confident thing you've ever done before. My confidence comes in waves, sometimes it's here for a long time and other times it's gone as quickly as it came. I've learned to lean into the moments it is present and make the most of those days. I try to worry less about the days it's not there, as those will pass.

I also teach my clients when it comes to social media, you control the number of times you are showing up based on what you can realistically maintain. Most marketing professionals will tell us to show up consistently, posting three or four times a day at peak times for "maximum conversion." I'm not like most marketing professionals. I will tell you that authenticity doesn't have a schedule or timeline; it flows freely from within when it is ready to come out and is often unscripted. If we are truly wanting to be our most authentic selves, I believe it is important that we allow ourselves the freedom to approach how we show up in a way that fits who we are. This also includes not showing up if we feel social media isn't right for us.

The beautiful thing about your life is that it is just that, yours. No one can define you or what you do. They can try, but ultimately, it's your choice to be who you want to be. In a world filled with critics, it's easy to want to be someone we aren't. In our pursuit to live a life filled with viral sensations and the latest trends, we often find ourselves straying further from discovering our true potential. In trying on someone else's lifestyle for size, we end up distancing ourselves even more from understanding who we truly are at our core.

In my life, I've tried to do what everyone else said to do. I bought the magic items that came straight to my doorstep the very next day, and I scrolled aimlessly as I compared myself to others. I wanted to stay hidden. I wanted to keep my life bottled inside, never sharing it with anyone, but something deep within said, *"Shonda, rise-up! It's your time to shine!"* So I did the unthinkable: I slayed the giant simply by showing up.

Take Back Your Power

My breakthrough came one morning after a good night's rest. I just woke up and told myself, *"No more! No more comparison, no more envy, no more jealousy, and certainly no more deception."* As scary as it felt, I had to be okay with not being a mother, not being thin, and not being enough for some people. I also had to work on being more patient and kinder towards those who seemed to enjoy making my life difficult. I knew that to fully embrace my most authentic self, I had to start living in a way that others could see me, no matter how vulnerable that made me.

So, I got up from my bed and faced myself in the mirror. While difficult to confront the woman staring back at me, I decided that I would help free her this time. Locking eyes with myself I repeated the statement *I am confident and capable* until I felt like I was more confident and capable. Slaying the giant of fear of rejection and humiliation doesn't mean that those things won't still happen. Instead, it means that I'm more prepared for them to happen and have put into place a strategy to help me deal with it head-on with confidence. Will it still hurt? Absolutely, but I'll rise-up, shake the dust off, and continue with my life with God by my side.

I have come to understand that fear may linger, always on the edge of our thoughts, ready to undermine our strides forward. In its shadow, we risk not fully embracing the richness of life. It's often us who play the role of the giants in our own stories, barricading ourselves behind the walls of apprehension towards the unseen. Yet, we overlook the truth that our journey has been divinely charted, that with God as our ally fear loses its grip. In moments overwhelmed by sadness, He is the architect of our joy.

You may be in a place where fear threatens to stop your progress. You may not feel ready to take a step forward just yet, and that's ok. You need to know that you are stronger and more resilient than you think. Draw nearer to God in the moments when you feel afraid and let Him help you get back out there again. I want you to know that it's going to be okay, no matter the outcome, because your life is worth living even when it looks differently than what you had envisioned.

We take our power back by slaying the giant before us with the tools given to us by God Almighty. Tools like faith, hope, and even love. I have found that even in my brokenness I can trust that God will use those shattered pieces of my heart to help others repair their hearts that have been broken. Your life, your story, your purpose—all of it can be used for the greater good of helping just one person who needs you to be your most authentic self.

Identity Struggle

In today's world, heavily influenced by social media, guarding our hearts and minds has become a battle ten times harder than it once was. Vulnerability leaves us exposed, our defenses lowered, hearts open, ripe for the enemy's taking. My journey with God has shown me a paradox: the deeper my commitment, the more I seem to attract trials and tribulations. There have been times these challenges overpowered me, dictating my actions. Yet, there were also times they became the soil from which my resilience, nurtured by prayer and God's guidance, grew stronger.

Every time I sat down to write this book or work on a chapter, something would happen around me or a negative thought would cross my mind making me want to give up, retreat, or flat out say no to finishing this book. Some days would go by and I wouldn't write because I was tapped out emotionally. But instead of retreating, I asked God to help me find the words, teach the lessons He wanted me to teach, and help me slay the giant of fear that stood before me in hopes that one person may find joy again by reading my story.

Friend, if you think back to the last week, how many times have you compared yourself to another? How about in the last month? Or what about over the past year? Take a moment to think over how many times you compared yourself to others and write it down. As you do, pay attention to your reaction. Are you surprised at the numbers on the page? Why or why not?

How often do you choose to retreat and hide, rather than seeking God's strength to conquer the giants before you?

Glimpses of Grace

In navigating life's battles, much like the story of David and Goliath, I see parts of myself in both roles. Sometimes I'm David, facing my giants with bravery. Other times, I feel more like Goliath, standing in my own way. Let's dive into scripture and read the story first hand:

David was the youngest. The three oldest followed Saul, but David went back and forth from Saul to tend his father's sheep at Bethlehem. For forty days the Philistine came forward every morning and evening and took his stand. Now Jesse said to his son David, 'Take this ephah of roasted grain and these ten loaves of bread for your brothers and hurry to their camp. Take along these ten cheeses to the commander of their unit. See how your brothers are and bring back some assurance from them. They are with Saul and all the men of Israel in the Valley of Elah, fighting against the Philistines.' Early in the morning David left the flock in the care of a shepherd, loaded up and set out, as Jesse had directed. He reached the camp as the army was going out to its battle positions, shouting the war cry. Israel and the Philistines were drawing up their lines facing each other. David left his things with the keeper of supplies, ran to the battle lines and asked his brothers how they were. As he was talking with them, Goliath, the Philistine champion from Gath, stepped out from his lines and shouted his usual defiance, and David heard it. Whenever the Israelites saw the man, they all fled from him in great fear. —1 Samuel 17:14–24

Grace is found in David's fearlessness. In a situation where others saw Goliath and fled, David remains. Much like David, when we stand before our giants, we must do so fearlessly, ready and willing to take action with God by our side.

David asked the men standing near him, 'What will be done for the man who kills this Philistine and removes this disgrace from Israel? Who is this uncircumcised Philistine that he should defy the armies of the living God?' They repeated to him what they had been saying and told him, 'This is what will be done for the man who kills him.' When Eliab, David's oldest brother, heard him speaking with the men, he burned with anger at him and asked, 'Why have you come down here? And with whom did you leave those few sheep in the wilderness? I know how conceited you are and how wicked your heart is; you came down only to watch the battle.' 'Now what have I done?' said David. 'Can't I even speak?' He then turned away to someone else and brought up the same matter, and the men answered him as before. —1 Samuel 17:26–30

Grace is found in David's passion for defending God's name and standing up for righteousness. Much like David, we may have found ourselves in situations where others don't allow us the chance to speak up or accuse us of doing something with ill intent. This can be extremely frustrating, but we need to defend God's name and stand up for righteousness just as David did.

David said to the Philistine, 'You come against me with sword and spear and javelin, but I come against you in the name of the Lord

Almighty, the God of the armies of Israel, whom you have defied. This day the Lord will deliver you into my hands, and I'll strike you down and cut off your head. This very day I will give the carcasses of the Philistine army to the birds and the wild animals, and the whole world will know that there is a God in Israel. All those gathered here will know that it is not by sword or spear that the Lord saves; for the battle is the Lord's, and he will give all of you into our hands.' So David triumphed over the Philistine with a sling and a stone; without a sword in his hand, he struck down the Philistine and killed him. —1 Samuel 17:45–47; 50

Grace is found in God guiding David in a very challenging situation while giving him the confidence and capability he needs to overcome the impossible—slaying the giant! Much like David, God also guides us in our challenging times. He equips us with what we need to be confident and capable in all situations.

The Heart of the Matter: You Were Created to Be You

Every challenge you've faced in life holds significance. Our greatest triumphs and our deepest valleys each carry lessons that shape us. It's through navigating these experiences we uncover our true selves.

You are uniquely crafted by God to be precisely who you are. He has laid out a path tailored just for you, a path only He fully comprehends. Yet, our human frailty sometimes sees us halted, faced with obstacles that loom on our journey. My friend, how long you allow the giant to keep you stuck is up to you. The decision to remain idle or to rise and conquer that giant of fear is yours. Each choice is valid, for you are under God's guiding hand.

Finding Joy

While taking a step out can bring uncertainty and vulnerability, be encouraged; it can also open doors for you that you never thought were possible. One way slaying my giant—fear of rejection and humiliation—

has knocked down the walls around my heart is in learning to love myself as God loves me. I'll share more about that in the next chapter.

The only thing you must do now is prepare your heart. I'm not asking that you put yourself back out there just yet, but that is coming soon. It is helpful to prepare your heart and mind before that moment comes so you can be prepared to step out in faith, with confidence, when the time is right. Joy is found when we courageously step forward and slay our giants.

Anchor Points

Rediscovering your authentic self and rebuilding your faith takes time. Be patient with yourself and trust that God will guide you through these exercises. Each one is meant to be an anchor point to help keep you authentically anchored in Christ.

Affirm

Write the following scripture somewhere you will see it daily. Memorize it, and refer to it when you lose faith in who you are.

> *"You make known to me the path of life; you will fill me with joy in your presence, with eternal pleasures at your right hand."* —Psalm 16:11

Prayer

Heavenly Father, I am often afraid and filled with feelings of anxiousness or worry that steal my peace. Thank you for the reminder that no matter what, no matter who I am, it's going to be ok. Lord, please help me to be brave as I lean into the possibility of becoming more my authentic self in you. Thank you, Lord, for helping me slay the giants before me, Amen.

Journal Prompt

I desire to be living in peace, therefore I will let go of...

_____

_____

_____

_____

_____

_____

_____

_____

_____

_____

_____

_____

_____

_____

_____

_____

_____

_____

_____

_____

_____

_____

_____

_____

_____

_____

_____

_____

_____

_____

_____

_____

Declaration Statements

"I am" statement: Write a statement about who you feel you are in this very moment. *Example: I am confident and capable.*

I am

_____

_____

"I hope to be" statement: Write a statement about who you hope to be by the end of this book. *Example: I hope to be my most authentic self always, without fear.*

I hope to be

_____

_____

chapter Thirteen
Love Yourself as God Loves You

Loving myself has always been a battle. How can I embrace self-love when it feels like others are swift to highlight my flaws, judging me solely on my exterior without ever understanding who I am? My weight has been a constant rollercoaster; I've experimented with every diet trend and poured money into supplements and protein powders. Yet, despite all my efforts, nothing seemed to bring the change I hoped for.

There was a time in my early twenties when I was thin, a direct consequence of battling anorexia. This struggle emerged after a close friend I deeply cared about told me I wasn't desirable because of my weight. When I was thin, it felt as though everyone suddenly wanted to listen to me, to be in my presence. Unfortunately, I soon found myself in the hospital. The fallout from dealing with an eating disorder resulted in destroying my metabolism which only further complicated matters for me as I packed on the pounds once I went back to eating regularly. It is an experience I long to forget, as it has left internal scars so deep, they are hard to hide.

I often wonder what my life would have looked like without the limitations I have when it comes to maintaining a healthy lifestyle—limitations I worry I caused with an eating disorder and limitations I was created with. I have always been vocal about being diagnosed with polycystic ovarian syndrome, and this has caused a massive struggle with losing weight like most normal people would. It wasn't from lack of trying. I've hired several personal trainers over the years and followed their plans as closely as I could only to gain weight and not lose any inches.

Frustrated, I sought out help from a medical professional who uncovered I have an allergy to gluten and dairy, as well as a myriad of other things. I've spent the last several years learning what foods I can and cannot eat, working on meal prep and planning each week, and trying my hardest to make choices that helped in my overall health instead of focusing so much on the number the scale reads. I wanted to truly understand my body and what helps it feel good versus what makes it tired or sluggish.

When grief was added to the mix, it further complicated things because most days I didn't want to eat anything and would quickly find myself falling back into old patterns that had negative consequences. The problem was I would lose weight and it wouldn't take long for someone to vocally point out the difference in my appearance, resulting in my mindset taking a nosedive.

When compliments on my changing appearance were voiced, they felt like stark reminders that my value was seen only in physical terms, overshadowing my inner qualities and capabilities. This perception hindered my progress, planting seeds of doubt about my worth unless I conformed to societal standards of appearance. Struggling with weight change intensified my self-disdain, as I struggled with not meeting these external expectations.

I didn't want to be this way, both externally and internally. I wanted to be happy, healthy, active, and energized. Once I decided I needed to fully embody my authentic self, I knew that meant I had to love who I was at the size I was. Others may not fully accept or embrace me because of my body image, but I knew that God would bring individuals into my life who were meant to love and support me as I deserve to be loved and supported. I also knew that for this to be successful, I had to stop listening to what others said—both the negative and the positive—about my appearance.

While I am far from perfect in the food I consume, I have made drastic lifestyle changes that have begun serving me well for a healthier future. I have learned to be patient with myself and my progress, as it looks different each day. When we talk about rebuilding our lives after hardship, it's important to remember everything takes time. It's ok to go at your own pace.

My Body is My Temple

What I have learned through the lifestyle changes I have made and through reading the Bible is that my body is my temple, and to keep it going, I must honor my temple the best I possibly can. By being purposeful in my approach to cherishing my temple, I am creating a space for God to enter wholly and begin to work within.

We could discuss all the things that my temple needs—fuel in the form of foods that give it energy and keep me alert; strength in the form of exercise that gives it flexibility and tone; and solitude in the form of meditation and prayer to help clear the mind from the negativity that often surrounds it—but this is all surface level.

Most days I still don't understand why my body is so different from most other people and why it's harder for me to lose weight. I do worry about how others perceive me and what they are saying, even though I know that I need to learn to love myself more, flaws and all. The negative self-talk that accompanies how I feel about my outward appearance isn't loving my temple, it's abusing it.

We are sometimes our worst critics. We tend to see ourselves in a negative light and get fixated on that instead of getting to the root of the issue. If my body is my temple, don't I owe it to myself to treat all of it better, including my thoughts about myself?

If every decision we make starts with determining how it will affect our temple, we may try to make better choices. The most important thing for you to remember is this: your body is your temple; it is not anyone else's. We have all grown accustomed to accepting unsolicited advice from those in our immediate circle, perhaps now is a good time to seek God's advice on how to treat your temple in a way that honors Him.

God Loves You

When we are going through hardship, or even after hardship has happened and we are in the rebuilding stage, it is hard to remember that God loves us. There were many times I questioned whether God did love me. There were situations I found myself in where acquaintances would speak ill of my appearance to me directly, and it would hurt so much that I didn't know if God loved me. I questioned Him almost daily.

I am just a woman who went through some pretty hectic stuff and did her best to make sense of it all. I knew what I had learned in Church about God, I knew what the Bible said about God, and I knew what my heart said about my relationship with God. I used the knowledge I had during my time in mediation and prayer to converse with God directly. I'd ask Him some hard questions, often through sobs and cries of agony. I would try to lay it all at the feet of Jesus and trust that He was helping me through it.

He has brought me up out of that dark water, placed my feet on solid ground, and helped me rebuild who I am in Him. That alone is all the proof I need to know that God loves me unconditionally, no matter what my weight is, or if I'm strong. Romans 8:38–39 tells us the magnitude of His love for us: *"For I am convinced that neither death nor life, neither angels nor demons, neither the present nor the future, nor any powers, neither height nor depth, nor anything else in all creation, will be able to separate us from the love of God that is in Christ Jesus our Lord."*

It's important to know that loving yourself as God loves you helps you to grow and lean more into your authentic self. When we live a life loathing our very existence, we cannot see the good that God has set before us, and we may miss out on opportunities because we shy away from others. God didn't create you for nothing; He created you for something. He created you to be the person you are today. You are trying, and He sees that and loves you more for it.

Identity Struggle

Your outward appearance isn't what defines who you are because there is far more to you than that. The only opinion when it comes to your body and appearance that matters is God's. Society has changed the way we treat others and is trending more negative every day. What another person says about your appearance holds zero weight in comparison to what God says.

When you choose to make changes that positively honor your body, it pleases God. He wants you to feel your best and to fulfill your calling. But, the only way you can do so is by trying. Additionally, your mind is also an important part of who you are. Working on changing those negative thoughts to be more positive and loving will help you become the best version of yourself.

We each live our lives differently. What I have found that works for me may not work for you, and vice versa. Everybody has a body, but every body is different. Dare to love yourself as God loves you.

How many times do you abuse your body in a way to fit into someone else's mold instead of honoring God in all you do to your body?

Glimpses of Grace

When it comes to honoring our bodies, I searched the Bible to find a story that felt relatable to the approach of how one may care for their body. What I found was the first chapter of Daniel. There was a specific portion of this chapter that stuck out to me, and I want to share it with you:

> But Daniel resolved not to defile himself with the royal food and wine, and he asked the chief official for permission not to defile himself this way. Now God had caused the official to show favor and compassion to Daniel, but the official told Daniel, 'I am afraid of my lord the king, who has assigned your food and drink. Why should he see you looking worse than the other young men your age? The king would then have my head because of you.' —Daniel 1:8–10

Grace is found when Daniel takes a stand to honor his body in a way that is pleasing to God. Much like Daniel, we too can choose to not defile ourselves with things that cause harm to our bodies. This doesn't just include food or beverage, as there are other bad habits we pick up along the way that contribute to our overall health and wellbeing. Making the effort is the first step in living a healthier life.

> *Daniel then said to the guard whom the chief official had appointed over Daniel, Hananiah, Mishael, and Azariah, 'Please test your servants for ten days: Give us nothing but vegetables to eat and water to drink. Then compare our appearance with that of the young men who eat the royal food and treat your servants in accordance with what you see.' So he agreed to this and tested them for ten days. At the end of the ten days, they looked healthier and better nourished than any of the young men who ate the royal food. So the guard took away their choice food and the wine they were to drink and gave them vegetables instead. To these four young men God gave knowledge and understanding of all kinds of literature and learning. And Daniel could understand visions and dreams of all kinds.* —Daniel 1:11–17*

Grace is found in the provisions God gave the four young men who followed a diet that might have seemed less appealing. Because Daniel was obedient and put God first when it came to honoring his body, God blessed the four of them with better health and appearance, as well as blessing them with gifts for their obedience.

Just like the four, we too can reap the blessings of being obedient by honoring our body. The more we consistently choose to put our self-care needs first, the better in the long run our bodies will perform. You have one life to live, so don't you want to live it in a way that serves God at your fullest capacity for as long as possible? I know I do, which is why I am prioritizing loving myself as God loves me.

The Heart of the Matter: You Are So Very Loved

Allow me to remind you: You are so very loved. Hardships are often hard on us emotionally, mentally, and physically. They can leave us debilitated for lengthy periods. When others pass along harsh judgments, no matter how lovingly they claim to do so, it is easy to let what they say cut us to our core and stop us from even trying to make better choices. You must be ready, willing, and able to instill change in your life that contributes to a healthier you, no one can force that issue for you.

As someone who has struggled with my weight and health my whole life, I have come to accept who I am and how my body was created. This doesn't mean I am content or happy with where I am physically, but it means that I have learned in order to achieve results for my body type, I must treat myself with more kindness and compassion.

While I always strive to maintain a healthy lifestyle, I'm not perfect, but I do challenge myself to make choices based on God's direction to honor my temple and Him. Loving yourself as God loves you is one of the hardest things you'll ever do, but it also helps you to establish new habits for a healthier you.

Finding Joy

No magic pill or diet will help you learn to love yourself more. You must do the work internally before you can see results externally. Our minds hold the power to set us up for success or knock us down in failure. I struggled with wanting to be more present socially due to my outward appearance, I'll share with you how I overcame that in the next chapter.

One of the best ways I can honor my temple is to choose to love it and extend grace when the number on the scale won't budge despite my pants fitting a little looser than usual. Bodies are complex, but one thing will always remain—God loves you. The more I made the right choices for my temple, the freer I felt as little by little the labels on the anchor chains no longer carried weight. Joy is found once you prioritize loving yourself as God loves you.

Anchor Points

Rediscovering your authentic self and rebuilding your faith takes time. Be patient with yourself and trust that God will guide you through these exercises. Each one is meant to be an anchor point to help keep you authentically anchored in Christ.

Affirm

Write the following scripture somewhere you will see it daily. Memorize it, and refer to it when you lose faith in who you are.

"Do you not know that your bodies are temples of the Holy Spirit, who is in you, whom you have received from God? You are not your own; you were bought at a price. Therefore, honor God with your bodies." —1 Corinthians 6:19–20

Prayer

Heavenly Father, I am so sorry for not loving myself as you love me. I have struggled to see what you see in me and have allowed the opinions of others to keep me captive in my mind. Lord, I ask for your help as I try harder to honor my temple so that I can honor you. Thank you, Lord, for giving me the strength to keep trying, Amen.

Journal Prompt

The way God has shown me how much He loves me is…

_____

_____

_____

_____

_____

_____

Declaration Statements

"I am" statement: Write a statement about who you feel you are in this very moment. *Example: I am strong and determined.*

I am

_____

_____

"I hope to be" statement: Write a statement about who you hope to be by the end of this book. *Example: I hope to be kinder to my temple.*

I hope to be

_____

_____

Chapter Fourteen

(Re)Build Your Community

Even though I am back on the shore, I have not magically discovered all the answers to becoming a flawless person. I have learned to give myself grace for my flaws and love myself a little more, as I strive to live a more Christ-centered life. I choose to focus on my relationship with God first and foremost because it is the most important thing I could do to better myself and my relationships.

During the season I found myself at the deepest depths of the ocean floor, my faith was far from what it once was. I had already stopped going to Church regularly, and the surging tides of grief, mixed with the need to protect the feelings of those around me, left me feeling unprepared. In this tough season, I made a decision for solitude which led to the straining of friendships that lacked the resilience to weather the storm of separation. I was acutely aware that I wasn't embodying my usual self, and to fulfill the role of a true friend, I needed to revert to the version they had grown familiar with. Yet, I found myself utterly drained, lacking the energy to squeeze back into that familiar mold any longer. I was in desperate need of this season of *prayerful solitude* to help me figure out who I was and what God was asking of me. God was removing people from my life that were meant to be removed to make room for the new ones who would be entering it when the time was right.

Eventually, when the time came to emerge from this season of solitude and invite others to join me in person again, I felt scared. But as I began to visit with others more frequently, I realized how much I missed everyone and was eager to spend as much time as possible with them again. I adopted the 'making up for lost time' mentality, yet I was aware that I had changed from who I was before. Unsure of how this new version of me would be received by others, I hesitated, holding back slightly before fully revealing this new aspect of myself.

I have a couple of friends who have graciously stuck with me through each season, giving me the space to be vulnerable and share my insecurities with them as they kept my words guarded. My life had gone from being a devout Christian woman serving in ministry, to a silenced woman struggling with her faith, and back to a more vocal Christian woman wanting to be in ministry again which is where I am today.

I hold the belief that we can all live together in harmony; perhaps that's somewhat naive, but I firmly believe that when we're instructed to 'love our neighbors as ourselves,' it encompasses loving everyone, devoid of judgment. I have friends who are Christians, just as I have friends who aren't, and I always want to be respectful of each of their personal beliefs while still honoring my own. Despite the challenge of refraining from judgment, it's crucial to strive even harder to lead with love and kindness. I'm aware that some of my friends might not read this book due to its religious themes, yet I'm confident they will support and encourage me as I venture out in faith and follow what I believe to be right. And with that, I am perfectly content. I cherish them in their most genuine and authentic forms, respecting their choice of religion as a personal decision they are fully entitled to make, just as I am with mine.

Over the years, I've grown to understand that change starts with me. This realization guides my approach to rebuilding my community, where I make deliberate choices about whom I welcome and how I support them. My aim is to be an encourager and a support system; I aspire to be chosen as someone's chosen family—to treat others with more kindness than I have received. I have a desire to develop my community with connections that go beyond the superficial, cultivating deep-rooted relationships where loved ones know they can find solace on my couch and in my embrace during their moments of sorrow. I recognize that safety and respect are mutual, and by setting an example through my actions, demonstrating the truth of my words, I trust that others will also engage more authentically with me.

Authenticity Attracts Authenticity

Authenticity is a major factor in rebuilding our community. When it comes to embodying our most authentic selves, we are presenting the most vulnerable and exposed aspect of who we are at our core. This reality can feel awkward and embarrassing at times, filled with concern over how others may perceive us, leading us to conceal this truest part of ourselves beneath a façade designed for protection. Authenticity means embracing the courage to be imperfect, to be messy in the presence of those who refrain from judging our chaos and choose to love us unconditionally.

We have gotten to the point as a society where it is better to share only the good parts of us with the world while we hide away the messy and bad parts off camera. As we scroll through the pristine photos of the happiest faces, we wish we had their lives and their belongings, and eventually, we may find we start to live our lives in a way that is indicative of someone else. Be honest, would you have still wanted that same viral refrigerator organizer had you not seen it on a video? I know I wouldn't have. It's not practical and it now sits at the bottom of the donate pile, a splurge that wasn't worth it.

It's important to note that being authentic doesn't mean we have to put every single thing happening in our lives on display for the entire world to see. Keeping your deepest thoughts and revelations reserved for those in your inner circle is a way to protect your heart, while also nurturing and strengthening those close relationships. This act of guarding our innermost selves doesn't mean we're not being authentic; in fact, it's quite the opposite. By carefully choosing how much you share publicly, you'll find yourself growing more confident in your social media presence, especially if you're stepping back into it after a break.

Then, as you start to reengage with social media, authenticity involves presenting your personality in its most genuine form, alongside sharing basic information that's crucial for others to understand about you. It's akin to approaching a first date or meeting someone for the first time, where you aim for both of you to gradually get acquainted in manageable increments. This method not only allows you to express yourself truthfully but also draws you closer with individuals similar to you, and who knows, perhaps a new best friend is out there, hoping to discover someone exactly like you at this very moment.

If we want others to love us when we are in our vulnerable and authentic state, we must reciprocate that same everlasting love back to them for being brave enough to be themselves with us. We all crave a connection that runs deep, so deep that when trials arrive, the connection cannot be swayed. The temptation to gossip can ruin a relationship quickly, which is why we should resist it even if it is forced into our conversation by someone else. In our attempt to fit in with the crowd, someone's feelings may get hurt. The side of the crowd you choose to be on should align with what you believe and who you are authentically.

My friend, I care about you, flaws and all. Your truest authentic self is the only version of you that matters the most. When you are at your most authentic self, you are the most vulnerable, honest, and real with yourself and others. I know it's scary to be in a place of authenticity when others reject you for who you are. I have lived that as a reality for a long time, but the biggest lesson I've learned is that for every person who cuts us down, there are three more standing there ready to build us back up if we allow them.

Developing Deep-Rooted Relationships

Community is important, especially a community of like-minded individuals with similar beliefs and values as you. Having a group of friends who are supportive of one another and offer encouragement is beneficial for us all. If you have found that, in the past, your community has struggled, perhaps there are some lessons in that waiting to be discovered. Setting boundaries with your community and ensuring they are upheld keeps everyone safe and happy. Have those kinds of talks early on if possible.

The reality in life is that people you love and trust will come and go in your life. This can happen due to reasons beyond your control or may be a result of something you said or did that you didn't mean to do. While you navigate the waves of grief, don't forget who is at the center of it all—you and God. Use what you have learned with your time spent in solitude with God to seek guidance on how to strengthen the bonds within your connections.

My approach to building deep-rooted relationships with my friends has changed over the years and in different seasons of my life. I haven't always been the authentically best friend that I know I could be, and

I have many regrets and lost relationships as a result. The hard lesson of losing someone I cared deeply about will always be with me. I will never tell a friend I'm too tired to talk in the middle of the night if they need me. Life is short, things happen that we would never imagine could happen, and the guilt that comes with watching a close friend be buried will haunt me forever.

I encourage you to pray for your friends just as you would pray for your needs. Love and honor them for who they are, just as you would hope they would love and honor who you are. Cheer them on when they have something they want to celebrate, even if that something can be triggering to you—like the birth of a baby. When differences arise, reconciliation should be the first thing you try, but if it cannot be reconciled right away, give them the space they need before pushing it when it's not ready. Own your mistakes, apologize as soon as you learn of your error, and make a conscious effort to not repeat the same mistake.

Most importantly, when your friend is in her bottom of the ocean moment, dig in and hold her head above water to help keep her from drowning. No one should leave a friend suffering alone to figure it out on her own; we all need our person, and you may be hers. By choosing to support her—despite the differences that may arise between you— she won't forget it, and in the end, she'll love you even more. Choose to check in with her often, even if she isn't in her bottom of the ocean moment. By choosing to reach out first, you'll show her you are invested in her well-being.

May you go forth and (re)build connections that serve you for many more years to come.

Identity Struggle

Being my most authentic self when it came to my friendships meant that I had to start making them a priority. Connection matters to me in that I recognize when I need the support of my friends to help me get through a difficult day or to sit and laugh with me about some of the silliest things. I am filled with joy when I am with those who love me unconditionally.

I knew that the only way my connections would last for the remainder of my life was if I began showing up for them as I had hoped they would show up for me. I needed to knock the expectations off of the table and cherish every single moment spent with them. We all crave connection, so why do we push it away when we find it?

I invite you to be intentional when you select those who you choose to rebuild with. By aligning yourself with individuals who support you in your most vulnerable state, you are also inviting them to be their most vulnerable with you. Dare to be someone's person, wholeheartedly and authentically you.

How many times do you refuse to be the first to reach out to a friend because you always feel like you are the only one to do so?

Glimpses of Grace

When I consider what it is like to help a friend during their bottom of the ocean moment, I also think about the story of Shadrach, Meshach, and Abednego—three friends with unshakable faith supported each other in their bottom of the ocean moment that had them physically in a fiery furnace. Unsure if they would survive, they held steadfast onto God's presence. Join me in the furnace with them:

Your Majesty has issued a decree that everyone who hears the sound of the horn, flute, zither, lyre, harp, pipe and all kinds of music must fall down and worship the image of gold, and that whoever does not fall down and worship will be thrown into a blazing furnace. But there are some Jews whom you have set over the affairs of the province of Babylon—Shadrach, Meshach and Abednego—who pay no attention to you, Your Majesty. They neither serve your gods nor worship the image of gold you have set up.' Furious with rage, Nebuchadnezzar summoned Shadrach, Meshach and Abednego. So these men were brought before the king, and Nebuchadnezzar said to them, 'Is it true, Shadrach, Meshach and Abednego, that you do not serve my gods or worship the image of gold I have set up?' —Daniel 3:10–14

Grace is found in the stance taken by the three friends that landed them before the king. Their steadfast faith in God was what they had become known for—a steadfast faith in which the three of them, together, demonstrate their most authentic selves. Much like this trio, we can be steadfast in our faith with our friends, gathering with them in faith and fellowship.

Shadrach, Meshach and Abednego replied to him, 'King Nebuchadnezzar, we do not need to defend ourselves before you in this matter. If we are thrown into the blazing furnace, the God we serve is able to deliver us from it, and he will deliver us from Your Majesty's hand. But even if he does not, we want you to know, Your Majesty, that we will not serve your gods or worship the image of gold you have set up.' Then Nebuchadnezzar was furious with Shadrach, Meshach and Abednego, and his attitude toward them changed. He ordered the furnace heated seven times hotter than usual and commanded some of the strongest soldiers in his army to tie up Shadrach, Meshach and Abednego and throw them into the blazing furnace. —Daniel 3:16–20

Grace is found in the response from the trio to the king. They do not defend or argue, they simply state their truth and stand united together, ready to suffer whatever may come their way. Much like how the trio responded in the face of adversity, our approach in how we handle conflict with others should be met with grace and kindness. This speaks truth to the matter in a way that isn't an argument. By extending grace to those who choose to persecute us for our beliefs or life choices, we aren't giving them the green light to continue the mistreatment, but rather we are responding in love with the hope that God will work on changing them while we choose to stand firmly in Christ.

Nebuchadnezzar then approached the opening of the blazing furnace and shouted, 'Shadrach, Meshach and Abednego, servants of the Most High God, come out! Come here!' So Shadrach, Meshach and Abednego came out of the fire, and the satraps, prefects, governors and royal advisers crowded around them. They saw that the fire had not harmed their bodies, nor was a hair of their heads singed; their robes were not scorched, and there was no smell of fire on them. Then Nebuchadnezzar said, 'Praise be to the God of Shadrach, Meshach and Abednego, who has sent his angel and rescued his servants! They trusted in him and defied the king's command and were willing to give up their lives rather than serve or worship any god except their own God.'—Daniel 3:26–28*

Grace is found in God's protection over the trio as they were in the blazing furnace. Much like the trio, God protects us and our hearts when it comes to facing trials by sending others to walk alongside us in strength and prayer. Grace is also found in the king's response to the miracle he had just witnessed. He saw his soldiers killed in the fire when they took the trio to it, yet he witnessed the trio walk out of the fire miraculously untouched, protected by the fourth man he saw. Much like the king's response, others' opinions and behaviors can change when they see firsthand the growth that you have shown after facing hardships.

The Heart of the Matter: Rebuilding Your Community

God doesn't want us to be alone. This is why fellowship is so very important. When we go through hardships, it is common to isolate ourselves and turn away from others (even family). A season of solitude helps us reconnect with ourselves and God, and a season of rebuilding helps us reconnect with those we may have pushed away.

It's natural to be hesitant when approaching someone you may have pushed away for fear of rejection. The best way to handle this is to lead with love and an apology and let them know why you disconnected from them and how much you've missed them. Be open and honest with them and ask for their forgiveness for hurting them. The worst thing that could happen is you'll receive a resounding "no" as the door of their friendship permanently closes. Don't lose hope; know that God will still protect you as you move forward in rebuilding a community that will be strong and long-lasting.

Finding Joy

You will know when you are ready to join others again in fellowship. Allow others the chance to be a part of your beautiful life because you have so much to share with the world. Even I am still working on rebuilding my community. It is something that takes time, but little by little, my circle keeps growing as God introduces me to new people. Pray that God will lead others into your life that will form lasting connections.

As you step out in faith again and become more vulnerable with others, you'll begin to feel the presence of joy begin to resurface. I share with you my rediscovery of joy in the next chapter. Joy is found the moment we begin fellowshipping with others again in a way that honors our authentic selves.

Anchor Points

Rediscovering your authentic self and rebuilding your faith takes time. Be patient with yourself and trust that God will guide you through these exercises. Each one is meant to be an anchor point to help keep you authentically anchored in Christ.

Affirm

Write the following scripture somewhere you will see it daily. Memorize it, and refer to it when you lose faith in who you are.

"Do nothing out of selfish ambition or vain conceit. Rather, in humility value others above yourselves, not looking to your own interests but each of you to the interests of the others." —Philippians 2:3–4

Prayer

Heavenly Father, I ask for forgiveness for my shortcomings in my friendships. I pray, Lord for strength and courage to step out again as I work on rebuilding connections. I pray that you bring to me those who you want to be in my life for many years to come. I pray, Father, that this time around, I can make these connections stick and last for the rest of my life. Thank you, Lord, for the beautiful souls you'll undoubtedly send my way, Amen.

Journal Prompt

The person I am choosing to be for my friends is…

_____
_____
_____
_____
_____
_____
_____
_____
_____
_____
_____
_____
_____

Declaration Statements

"I am" statement: Write a statement about who you feel you are in this very moment. *Example: I am an authentic friend.*

I am

_____

_____

"I hope to be" statement: Write a statement about who you hope to be by the end of this book. *Example: I hope to be an encouragement to those who need me to be.*

I hope to be

_____

_____

Chapter Fifteen
Rediscovery of Joy

Restoring my happiness has always been a daunting challenge for me, one that I've faced countless times without success. I've often wondered why attaining happiness seemed so unattainable. Each time I believed I had grasped it fully, despair would soon follow, leaving me questioning once again. Over time, I've come to understand that happiness is a fleeting emotion, influenced by the situations and circumstances we encounter. Take, for instance, the moment I thought I found a paint shade I was convinced would be ideal for my living room, only to realize upon application that it was entirely wrong for the space. This scenario exemplifies how quickly our emotions can shift from happiness to frustration, highlighting the passing nature of happiness based on external factors.

I thought that once I reached a level of pure happiness it would mean all was right in my world and nothing could ever change that for me. What I didn't realize was that what I needed was to rediscover joy, not happiness, to fulfill this longing I had. It was joy that I sought, and joy comes from within and can be present even in the direst of situations through prayer and petition with God. It is sustained through challenges and shows us our resiliency. An example of this is when I stepped back and admired the latest color sample for the front room watching as the sun cast a warm glow across it. This is when I immediately knew it was the right color selection. This filled my heart with joy. In this example, we see how my mindset has shifted to one that is more hopeful and happier.

I thought I had settled on my final paint colors, only to find that as time progressed and I saw the samples in the various levels of lighting throughout the day, it simply wasn't working as I hoped. Off to the paint store I went and then back home with another stack of paint chips to compare the various shades of gray, blue, and taupe to match the light gray I selected for the living room and the white I chose for the kitchen. I was extremely frustrated that my time spent learning color theory didn't prepare me for the overwhelming task of finalizing paint colors for the walls of my home. I was a pro at choosing colors that compliment each other, so why did this process feel so hard?

My analysis paralysis had kicked into overdrive, causing me to be unable to make a final decision on the remaining rooms that were to be painted. I had taped up several potentials in each of the rooms on the main floor with hopes of deciding quickly so we could begin painting on Memorial Day weekend, which was just around the corner. I refused to put this task off any longer as six months had already passed from when I brought home the original paint chips. Mike and I both agreed now was the time.

Meanwhile, I had to take a step back to figure out why this experience was creating such a feeling of anxiousness. Wasn't I happy that I was finally going to paint these tired walls? I figured once I decided to proceed, everything would fall into place and *poof*, happiness restored. However, my nerves were telling me this was a bigger change than I realized since this process would inevitably be erasing history from my walls.

Unlocking Joy

The walls still carried the memories of what once was and what could have been. For example, the impossible red stain under the windows that I remember scrubbing tirelessly but could not remove completely. Looking at this stain I recalled the first week the kids were in our home and one of them dropped their cup splashing liquid everywhere. It was one of those moments where time freezes as the red liquid hits your white curtains and everything else around it and you know it's going to create an impossible stain. I had a choice at that moment, to react harshly by scolding them for their carelessness; or to show kindness, smiling as I cleaned it up and letting them know that accidents happen. I chose to take the kindness route and went so far as to praise the artistic outcome of the red splattered curtains. It was a life lesson I know I'll never forget, and wherever they are today, I pray they carry this positive memory with them as well.

So here I was, memories of the past bubbling up as I faced these walls. I decided to give myself a day to sit in my emotions about making the changes and remember the stories like the red splashes. I reminded myself that while change is hard, it contributes to my healing. This day marked eight years since they left our home. It occurred to me that they have lived as many years away from us as they were the age when they came to us as such, I knew it was time to get up off the couch and paint the walls.

I could feel God nudging me to make this change. It was important that I trust Him in this process—trusting He would bring me through it and to the other side. Most people wouldn't think twice about selecting paint colors for their homes, but this wasn't as simple as that. This was about more than walls. It was about erasing the visible memories that remained of years past.

Final decisions were made, and we began by painting the living room first. I have to tell you that I was surprised as Mike decided to go all in on this remodel and paint the ceilings too. I worried it may be too hard for us to do ourselves, which was in the end but was also so worth it. On the first day of painting, we didn't get as far as we had hoped because it took longer than expected due to deciding to paint the ceiling in our project. The second day, we kept our momentum and got paint on all of the walls. We went to bed exhausted, unsure of how we would find the strength to finish the trim on a third day—remember, we had a deadline of Memorial Day looming over us.

The final morning, I walked down the stairs to my jumbled living room with newly painted walls and was met with something I didn't expect: tears. I filled my coffee cup and sat on the couch gazing out our windows to the fountain flowing rhythmically atop the pond. Mike and I talked for a short time before we got back to work. We were thankful for the decision we made to change the look of the living room and excited to see how the other rooms would turn out. The living room felt different, lighter and happier as if the house was saying thank you for taking care of me. I realized then how joy can be rediscovered when we choose to do the hard things that promote growth within.

If you had told me when I was at the bottom of the ocean that painting my house would play such an important role in unlocking my joy, I would have thought you were lying. There was no way I could have comprehended how one small action would lead to such significant internal results for me. I have come to realize, when I am filled with joy, I am naturally happier.

Over the next two months, we painted a new room each weekend with the hopes of being able to present our hard work to our family at the end of October. With just one more coat of paint to go, I took a step back and admired the huge transformation that occurred in our home, particularly in our kitchen, and smiled. Several years prior, I had purchased a cobalt blue iridescent tile backsplash from a tile maker in New York, which was a big investment. We put it up when we got it but never finished the kitchen because shortly after we installed it—I had my miscarriage. This fresh change of color from tan to white had dramatically transformed the look of our kitchen causing my beautiful backsplash to shine. This was a joy-filled reminder I needed to finish strong and get the final coat on the walls.

Here Comes Gratitude

We finished painting and began hanging the window furnishings just in time for our Halloween gathering of friends and family. On the day of the party, standing in the space between the living room and kitchen, I opened our curtains and bamboo shades so I could see everything together. I was overcome by emotion; I had no idea our home could look as beautiful as it did in that moment.

I wept, and I thanked God for never giving up on me when I was tired and worn and for gently guiding me to get up off the couch and take action on the road to taking back my life. I am so grateful for going "all in" on me when I did because it allowed me the chance to change. I have learned through this experience. When we are unhappy with our life and the direction it is going, one of the best ways to turn it around is to do something that can bring us back to a place of gratitude.

My friend, facing difficult circumstances can feel overwhelming, but the isolation that comes from navigating hardships alone—especially when judgment is passed—compounds the struggle. This can be likened to the wear on my dingy walls; over time, the harsh thoughts and judgments of others can leave us feeling bruised and battered. Amidst these trials, feelings of unworthiness and negative self-talk can emerge. Yet, the remarkable truth remains: God's love for us is unfailing.

May we never take for granted the joy we've rediscovered through finding the purpose of our pain. If I can help one person know that what they are feeling because of their pain is completely normal and that there is hope on the other side of it, then I have fulfilled my purpose.

Time is irrelevant when it comes to landing in a place of gratitude after hardship. We all grow and change at our own pace; there is no right or wrong way. There is no perfect timetable for growth either. You will arrive at this place when you are ready, and God will be there waiting for you with open arms as you finally see it, finally know it, and finally feel Him in it all.

Identity Struggle

When I was so focused on trying to restore happiness, I failed to feel the joy within me. Getting these two things mixed up caused a series of confusion and disappointment when time after time I would end my day more frustrated than I began. I was bound and determined that happiness was what I needed to feel as though I had reached the destination I intended. Not feeling happy caused me to be confused and question what I was doing wrong when I was still not feeling it.

I realized that by making joy a constant state of mind, instead of focusing on trying to change my emotion to happiness, my mindset began to shift, and the way I thought and spoke changed too. In every situation I was faced with, seeking out joy made my struggles somehow feel smaller.

It's easy for us to want to force a change of emotion, no one wants to be in an uncomfortable place for a long period. Sometimes we have to step back and look at the bigger picture, or in my case the whole area, before God can show us what has always been right before us the whole time. Don't be too hard on yourself in this moment of truth, recognize what is around you, and make the choice for a change in mindset to allow joy to fully reside within you, starting now.

How many times do you push yourself to be happy instead of living a joy-filled life in Christ?

Glimpses of Grace

Emerging from hardship marks the beginning of truly living again. We are embracing change—often without even realizing it—by navigating through pain and allowing God to be by our side. Your steadfast faith and devotion to God pave the way for a renewal of joy, as modeled by Job. I encourage you to explore his entire story in the Bible (found in the book of Job). I want to highlight a crucial moment in his journey where we can discover grace, offering us valuable insights for our own lives. Let's discover grace together:

> *After Job had prayed for his friends, the Lord restored his fortunes and gave him twice as much as he had before. All his brothers and sisters and everyone who had known him before came and ate with him in his house. They comforted and consoled him over all the trouble the Lord had brought on him, and each one gave him a piece of silver and a gold ring. The Lord blessed the latter part of Job's life more than the former part. He had fourteen thousand sheep, six thousand camels, a thousand yoke of oxen and a thousand donkeys. And he also had seven sons and three daughters. The first daughter he named Jemimah, the second Keziah, and the third Keren-Happuch. Nowhere in all the land were there found women as beautiful as Job's daughters, and their father granted them an inheritance along with their brothers.*

After this, Job lived a hundred and forty years; he saw his children and their children to the fourth generation. And so Job died, an old man and full of years. —Job 42:10–17

Grace is found when God restores all to Job in abundance after his time of suffering. Much like Job, we may find that God also restores all in abundance to us after our hardships. To get to the place of restoration, we must first persevere in faith, trusting that God's grace can and will use our difficulties as opportunities for blessings later in life. If we give up along the way, we stop the natural progression of God's plan for us which can further delay us in fulfilling our purpose. Perseverance can be found within you gradually, with each step you take toward your goals.

The Heart of the Matter: Joyful Heart

The Lord blessed me by helping me rediscover my joy after I was obedient and followed the nudge to get up out of the recliner and stop living a life on autopilot, taking action as I worked hard to begin living life again. By applying the practices I've shared throughout this book, I rediscovered true joy once again.

He can do the same for you if you allow Him to work miracles within you. It will not just fall in your lap, action produces results. So if you long to rediscover joy, you must take action and do the things that God is nudging you to do, no matter how impossible it may feel.

Finding Joy

Remain steadfast in your faith as you endure trials. God will bless you with even greater prosperity and joy in the end. As you long for a happier life, remember that happiness is a fleeting emotion, but joy is a state of being that can be rediscovered through faith, obedience, and gratitude. God authentically created you and wants you to experience unending joy. I will share how you can now begin the joyful process of rebranding your life in the next and final chapter. Joy is found when you step back and look at the bigger picture, allowing God to show you His hand in all that lay before you.

Anchor Points

Rediscovering your authentic self and rebuilding your faith takes time. Be patient with yourself and trust that God will guide you through these exercises. Each one is meant to be an anchor point to help keep you authentically anchored in Christ.

Affirm

Write the following scripture somewhere you will see it daily. Memorize it, and refer to it when you lose faith in who you are.

"Consider it pure joy, my brothers and sisters, whenever you face trials of many kinds."—James 1:2

Prayer

Heavenly Father, I am so grateful for all you have done to help me get out of the bottom of the ocean and back on solid ground. I am so thankful for the lessons you've shown me along the way and the purpose you've given me in all of my pain. Thank you for reminding me that joy is present within me even during my most difficult times, that it never leaves me and is always there waiting for me to discover it again. Thank you, Lord, for opening up my heart and allowing me the chance to feel pure joy again, Amen.

Journal Prompt

Today I experienced joy in…

_____

_____

_____

_____

_____

_____

_____

_____

_____

_____

_____

_____

_____

_____

_____

_____

_____

_____

_____

_____

_____

_____

_____

_____

_____

_____

_____

_____

_____

Declaration Statements

"I am" statement: Write a statement about who you feel you are in this very moment. *Example: I am filled with joy.*

I am

_____

_____

"I hope to be" statement: Write a statement about who you hope to be by the end of this book. *Example: I hope to be joyful in all I do.*

I hope to be

_____

_____

Chapter Sixteen
You Are Authentically Created

When I was so focused on pleasing others, I stopped living life in a way that was pleasing to God. I was miserable, grouchy, and unkind on almost all days. I had to remember that life is worth living in a way that is pleasing to God, as well as to myself. If I was choosing to do things that brought me grief instead of joy, I was only contributing to my misery. I do not blame anyone but myself for the state I lived life in because no one told me to live it this way; I chose to.

When I live life in my most authentic way, I am kinder, more helpful, encouraging, and supportive, and while I am not a comedian, I do try to be fun. Authenticity feels joyful. If you are struggling with an identity crisis of your own, I encourage you to embrace your authenticity—even if you believe that version of you is unlovable due to the lies the enemy has told you. You are the most lovable at your most authentic self.

How many times do we stop being the person God created us to be in order to please others?

I used to be someone filled with high energy who spoke way too fast when sharing my passions. I have always been a bit too candid, speaking whatever was on my mind without holding back, both good and bad. I trusted people I met until they did something to prove they were untrustworthy. I honestly don't know why I was this way, but I do know that how I used to be is no longer how I am today.

Life's trials can so alter our view of the world that clarity seems hard to grasp until the mist clears. My journey felt like emerging from the ocean's depths where the prolonged darkness rendered the shore's bright light overwhelming, complicating my ability to see and understand my own reflection.

The labels of being "overly dramatic," "too sensitive," and "too much to handle" have echoed through my life, initially voiced by friends and eventually, hauntingly, by myself. These words shackled me with doubt, convincing me that my fundamental traits left me unworthy of love.

This belief seemed validated as I faced disappointments and desertions from those I leaned on in my darkest hours. I've struggled with an overwhelming sense of brokenness, feeling like an outcast not just for my physical struggles but for being deemed odd and cast aside.

There were moments here and there when I felt at ease with others, allowing my true self to emerge, and these were the times I felt genuinely joyful, embracing who I was unreservedly. Yet, almost as soon as I revealed my authentic self, doubt would creep in, and I'd retract, dimming my light so I remained unseen. This self-censorship led me to morph into someone I believed others would prefer, a version of myself that was unrecognizable even to me. Putting on this constant act felt like the only option—avoiding criticism or disapproval and convincing myself that this was somehow acceptable.

As a result, somewhere along the way, I started to believe that to be loved, I had to act a certain way or do what others asked of me, and so this is precisely what I did. I worked in a career that was unfulfilling and so far from what I felt I should be doing in life because I didn't believe in my potential before, but eventually, I decided to change that. But even then, I listened as I was told that the work I did wasn't a real job and didn't matter and I took it on the chin when coworkers determined I didn't have the qualifications that I did have. I allowed society to tell me that because I wasn't a mother I would never live a fulfilled life and I bought into the lie that nobody cared about what I had to say. Each lie was stacked on top of the one before it blocked out the person I had always wanted to be as she hid behind them.

I've always been a 'yes' girl. Whenever someone needed something, my response was an automatic yes, despite my inner desire to decline. This habit of prioritizing others' happiness over my own has been a longstanding pattern in my life. A common misunderstanding was that my lack of children somehow equated to having ample time and resources to meet others' expectations. I recall a specific instance when this assumption was voiced directly to me, leaving me stunned and silently questioning the audacity of the belief that my childlessness implied I had no personal commitments or life of my own.

Gradually, I began to assert myself, learning to say "no" when requests conflicted with my own plans or needs. Running a business demanded my full attention, and despite any skepticism about its legitimacy, I knew the success of my business depended solely on my effort. This shift towards setting boundaries wasn't well-received by friends used to my immediate availability for their conveniences. It's no wonder I faced an identity crisis in my forties, having spent so much time masquerading as someone I wasn't, all in the effort to meet others' expectations.

The Time is Now

Overtime, running my business became a catalyst for me to embrace my true self as it was crafted to reflect my core identity authentically. My mission, vision, and values are all things that I believe in, live by, and have memorized. Every choice I make is mine to do so. It is the first time I ever caught a glimpse of the girl who has been hiding behind the stack of lies, and I wanted to see her more.

I have gained confidence and started letting loose a little and allowing my personality to come through again. I have only been vulnerable with Mike and a few close friends because they allow me to be my weird and quirky self with them, and they always tell me how much they love who I was in my silliest moments. I finally feel ready to shake things up, to drop the act and stop pretending so I can begin to live in my skin and be happy about it, and so, my friend, here we are to the present day.

There comes a time when believing all the lies the enemy uses against us must stop, and that time is now. God has authentically created me to be filled with emotions so intense that I can feel the pain others carry and help them navigate their inner turmoil. He has given me the drive to be a leader and a steward for Him by boldly sharing my bottom of the ocean moment with others, no matter how hard it has been for me to do. God has assured me that all the pain I have endured does matter and that it will help others when I share with them the way that I have overcome all that threatened to destroy my very existence.

I am no longer worried or wondering what my purpose is or why things had to happen the way they did; instead, I have come to accept my life as it is and the choices I have made to get here. The things that happened in my past are there to remain, they may have tried to keep me down, but they were unsuccessful in their attempt. I have taken ownership of my life and the direction it will head in the future by bringing God in to help guide me there.

When I first felt the nudge to write this book, I laughed and said, "nope, not doing it." A few weeks went by and there was the nudge again, and then again, and then again, until I finally said, *Okay, God, if I agree to write it, will you leave me be?!* I'm so glad that I heeded the nudge and sat down to plan out every detail because writing this book has unlocked so many lessons I was too afraid to see. Having emerged from the depths, I can see God lovingly standing behind me in this season, graciously carrying the weight of my anchor ensuring I won't drift out to sea again.

God's plan for my life is far different from what I had mapped out for myself. My vision included a large, loving family, rich in respect who treasure sharing time and memories together. Yet, what God has blessed me with is a beautiful mosaic of individuals, friendships from every walk of life, who show me love, offer respect, and find joy in simple gatherings around pizza boxes, jars of pickles, and gourmet brownies. This reality, surpassing anything I could have envisioned, signals there's still more to unfold.

Accept Yourself

Embracing authenticity begins with accepting ourselves as we are, a task far easier said than done. Confronted with the challenge I'd long avoided, I stood before a full-length mirror. There, I scrutinized every aspect of my appearance, especially those features others had criticized. My gaze lingered on what they deemed flaws: wide hips, pronounced thighs, a double chin, soft rolls, the gap between my teeth, my uneven smile, and untamed hair.

I spent a long while in front of the mirror, turning this way and that, taking in every detail of myself. It wasn't until my gaze finally met my own in the mirror that I noticed the tears that had silently fallen. My eyes, a deep, sorrowful green, always seemed their most striking when I was sad. With a tentative smile, I softly told my reflection, "I accept and love myself as I am, authentically created by God."

Loving myself began when I started to love myself as God loved me, but accepting myself for who I am began at that moment I shared above. It was as if I had stripped back all the false personas I had put on before so that I could be the person God created me to be all along.

As I sit here staring at the page before me, I can see the twinkling lights on our Christmas tree just beyond me in the front room, and I am reminded that I was created and anchored in God for a time such as this. As simple as it sounds, it is so fulfilling and rewarding to know that God has brought me from a place of darkness where all hope felt lost and breathed new life into me this year. The number of tears that I have shed while writing this book has washed away the shame and guilt that I have carried for most of my life as I give it all to God.

There's hope, my friend. He can work wonders in your life just as He has in mine. I understand that each of our journeys is unique, and what was manageable for me might pose a challenge for you. The specifics of our situations don't overshadow the fact that God transcends them all. He is just as present for you as He has been for me. Your true self awaits, ready for you to embrace who you are.

Glimpses of Grace

Having become unrecognizable to myself and others is when I realized I was living a life that wasn't true to who I was. This reminds me of the life of Joseph. As always, I encourage you to read the full story found in Genesis chapters 37 to 50, but I am going to take a closer look at some moments where the core of his identity came into question. Let's take a look together:

Now Joseph was the governor of the land, the person who sold grain to all its people. So when Joseph's brothers arrived, they bowed down to him with their faces to the ground. As soon as Joseph saw his brothers, he recognized them, but he pretended to be a stranger and *spoke harshly to them. 'Where do you come from?' he asked. 'From the land of Canaan,' they replied, 'to buy food.' Then he remembered his dreams about them and said to them, 'You are spies! You have come to see where our land is unprotected.' But they replied, 'Your servants were twelve brothers, the sons of one man, who lives in the land of Canaan. The youngest is now with our father, and one is no more.—* Genesis 42:6–10*

Grace is found when Joseph can recognize his brothers, despite them not recognizing him and remembering the details of his dream. Much like Joseph, we can recognize ourselves again with the help of God.

Then Joseph could no longer control himself before all his attendants, and he cried out, 'Have everyone leave my presence!' So there was no one with Joseph when he made himself known to his brothers. And he wept so loudly that the Egyptians heard him, and Pharaoh's household heard about it. Joseph said to his brothers, 'I am Joseph! Is my father still living?' But his brothers were not able to answer him, because they were terrified at his presence. Then Joseph said to his brothers, 'Come close to me.' When they had done so, he said, 'I am your brother Joseph, the one you sold into Egypt! And now, do not be distressed and do not be angry with yourselves for selling me here, because it was to save lives that God sent me ahead of you.'— Genesis 45:1–5*

Grace is found when Joseph unveils his true identity to his brothers, not with resentment but with forgiveness, attributing the preservation of lives to God's divine plan. Despite his trials, Joseph's story teaches us about the power of authenticity, forgiveness, and acknowledging God's role in our hardships. By embracing our genuine selves and recognizing God's work in our lives, we too can impact others positively, echoing Joseph's testimonial of faith and resilience.

The Heart of the Matter: Living Life Authentically

Your past events are unchangeable, yet your attitude towards their impact on your identity is within your control. Forgiveness is the secret to authentic living—forgiveness of others, God, and, crucially, oneself. While forgiving others might come more easily, self-forgiveness presents a greater challenge. Yet, it is through forgiveness that we find a pathway to true redemption, unlocking our ability to live genuinely and fully. Embracing forgiveness paves the way for a life led authentically, shedding the burdens of past grievances to step into a more honest and liberated existence.

It's easy to say we will do something, but the real challenge is in taking action reminiscent of the business principle of "know, like, and trust." We also have a like, know, and trust factor that each person we meet will consider when it comes to being in our community. To genuinely connect and be valued for your uniqueness and to earn trust, you must actively engage in authentic self-presentation. Show up genuinely to elevate your personal "know, like, and trust" factor.

When you are ready to rebrand and share your authenticity with the world, it is my prayer that you will go boldly and confidently, allowing God to shine His light through all you say and do.

It's Time to Rebrand

Congratulations my friend! You've reached a pivotal moment where it's time to reintroduce yourself to the world in your truest form. It's time for you to *rebrand*. What exactly does this mean for you? It signifies you're prepared to let the world see the real you, in all your uniqueness and authenticity.

This is when it gets fun! It reminds me of a newborn deer when they try to stand for the first time and their legs are all wobbly, but they are excited to try out walking. Sure, they may fall once or twice, but it doesn't take long for them to hop and run away confidently.

In rebranding your life, I recommend utilizing a process like the process I use to lead my clients through branding their business. First, start by creating a mood board, saving visuals that speak to you in this new season of life. Next, once you've gathered all your inspiration, go through your board, and make notes of the themes that you see beginning to take shape. The only thing left to do now is share who you are with others. Naturally, this process takes much longer when it's our life we are rebranding but the concepts are the same.

You can embrace your authentic self gradually, incorporating your identity into daily life and genuine relationships. This transition can reflect in your actions, interactions, social media presence, habits, hobbies, relationships, and even personality. Start by infusing your authentic identity into everyday activities as a constant reminder of who you truly are.

When it comes to social media, you may discover that those you currently follow no longer fit into your lifestyle. You are allowed to do a total purge, or a social media makeover. Some of the healthy changes I made were to begin following more faith-based social media accounts and ridding myself of accounts that posted negativity. I didn't stop with just social media; I also did a complete makeover of my home library by donating books that no longer aligned with who I was becoming and instead filled my bookshelf (or eBook reader) with books that covered more positive topics supporting my fresh outlook.

Another aspect of your transformation might involve rebranding your living space. As you start this journey of rebranding and you anchor yourself authentically, you might discover various areas within your home no longer resonate with your new identity. There's no need to overhaul everything at once; instead, approach this transition with ease, focusing on changes that feel right for you and align with your lifestyle preferences. This gradual approach ensures that your environment reflects your evolving identity without overwhelming you.

The primary areas to focus on for your life rebrand are your faith, your mindset, your actions, and your words. How you think will help you develop healthy habits, strengthen your faith in God, and speak encouragement to yourself and others. Change within you should come from a place of understanding and acceptance of who God is calling you to be. I pray you'll find the courage to share with others just how wonderful you are.

My friend, you should be so proud of yourself right now. You have gone on a journey from the depths of the ocean to rediscovering your identity in this new wave of life. You have put in the hard work of instilling new habits that helped you draw closer to God. When you are ready to reintroduce yourself to the world, please tag me in any social media posts you may share as a result of reading this book. I want to celebrate your emerging from the depths of the ocean floor as you launch back into the life God has for you! Remember you are authentically anchored in God. He uniquely created you for such a time as this. I encourage you now to live your life in faith, fellowship, and love.

Social Media tag: @shondaramseyofficial

Use hashtag: #authenticallyanchored

Anchor Points

Rediscovering your authentic self and rebuilding your faith takes time. Be patient with yourself and trust that God will guide you through these exercises. Each one is meant to be an anchor point to help keep you authentically anchored in Christ.

Affirm

Write the following scripture somewhere you will see it daily. Memorize it, and refer to it when you lose faith in who you are.

"But in your hearts revere Christ as Lord. Always be prepared to give an answer to everyone who asks. You to give the reason for the hope that you have. But do this with gentleness and respect." —1 Peter 3:15

Prayer

Heavenly Father, we have gone on a journey together from the depths of despair to joy-filled living. Lord, I am excited to be able to start living my life more authentically in a way that is pleasing to you. I pray for strength and guidance as I find my footing during my rebrand. Thank you, Lord, for revealing who I am in you, Amen.

Journal Prompt

Who I am at my most authentic is…

_____

_____

_____

_____

_____

_____

_____

_____

_____

_____

_____

_____

_____

_____

_____

_____

Declaration Statements

"I am" statement: Write a statement about who you feel you are in this very moment. *Example: I am my most authentic self.*

I am

_____

_____

"I hope to be" statement: Write a statement about who you hope to be by the end of this book. *Example: I hope to be a beacon of light to others so that they can find their way out of the bottom of the ocean.*

I hope to be

_____

_____

Acknowledgements

So Very Grateful

First and foremost, I want to express gratitude to Mike, whose unwavering support and understanding made the creation of this book possible. As my husband, you stood by me through the emotional rollercoaster of writing, the sleepless nights, and the fluctuating moods that accompanied me as I worked to meet deadlines. Your belief in me, especially during moments of self-doubt, fueled my determination to see this project through. I am forever thankful for your loving presence during the years I spent in autopilot mode, gently guiding me towards a future filled with joy. Growing old with you is my greatest blessing and honor.

To my children, our outcome didn't unfold as any of us hoped, but the lives you are now creating are proof that you are exactly where you were meant to be all along. Serving as your foster mom for two years of your childhood was an honor, one that enriched my life in countless ways. Through our time together, you taught me invaluable lessons about self-discovery, empathy, and the power of love. As you navigate the joys and challenges of parenthood, may the love we shared continue to uplift you. You are always in my thoughts and prayers.

To my family, thank you for filling my life with beautiful memories that still warm my heart today. I recognize that I haven't always been the easiest to rein in, with my wild ideas and big emotions, but your love and support throughout the years is irreplaceable. A special thank you to my mom for her assistance in the final stages of this book, carefully reviewing the proofs to ensure its readiness for print. Witnessing your expertise in the printing process come full circle as you supported my publishing experience has been very meaningful for me. Your passion for art has shaped my own, guiding me throughout my career and creative endeavors.

To Jamie, expressing my gratitude feels like an understatement for all you've done and continue to do for me. You cracked open my heart and brought out my love for writing, which had been buried deep under the surface. Writing with you has been not only fun but also freeing, and I look forward to the many more stories we write and share with each other. Thank you for fearlessly diving into my messy manuscript and helping me recognize its potential. You, my friend, are an extremely talented writer, and I eagerly await the day when you courageously share your gift with the world. I'll be the first in line to celebrate every book you publish.

To all my Friends, your unwavering support, encouragement, prayers, laughter, and tears have meant the world to me. I am forever grateful for how you have embraced my authentic self over the years. A special shoutout goes to Amanda, Carrie and Jake, Tracy, Susan and Jason, Megan, December, Morgan, Andrea, Heather, Crystal, Melissa, and Megan, for always knowing just how to lift my spirits on days when I didn't even realize I needed it. I look forward to the moments ahead when we'll continue to nurture and grow our deep-rooted friendships.

Thank you to April and Sarah for your uplifting mail during the writing process. Your cards and messages gave me the strength and determination I needed to see my book through to completion. Debbie and Scott, your efforts made my fortieth truly memorable, and your enduring friendship means the world to Mike and me. To the many others not mentioned by name, each of you has played a vital part in shaping my journey, and for that, I am deeply thankful.

To Krissy Nelson, my gratitude knows no bounds for your invaluable assistance in bringing this book to life. As an exceptional author coach, you guided me in translating the thoughts in my mind into the heartfelt message within my soul, in a manner I never thought possible. Your expertise in the developmental editing phase encouraged me to open my heart wider, share more deeply, and embrace my emotions.

Thank you for never letting me quit, for covering me in prayer, and for being my friend through it all.

To Amber Parr Burdett, your support and positivity have been a constant ray of sunshine for me throughout this whole process. I am grateful to have you by my side throughout this entire journey. I am extremely grateful to you for pouring your expertise into this book during the copy editing phase, ensuring it's ready for print. Our collaboration has been a joy, and I look forward to the continued growth of our friendship in the years to come.

To Larry Powell, your presence is deeply missed, but your legacy lives on in the hearts of many. I am immensely grateful for the warmth of your hospitality and the wisdom you imparted during our time together. As my mentor, you instilled in me invaluable lessons and sowed seeds of faith. Your trust in God continues to guide me on my journey, and I am forever thankful for your devotion to the Lord.

And to Jesus, thank you for giving your life so that I may live mine more abundantly. Thank you for extending your hand into the depths of the ocean, drawing me to the shore, and steadfastly holding my anchor in place, ensuring I never find myself adrift again.

About Authentically Created

Whether you're making your debut as an author or a seasoned storyteller, Authentically Created is here to support you as you publish your book. Authentically Created is an Independent Publishing Agency for Indie Authors.

Founded in 2024 by Shonda Ramsey, Authentically Created is here to help you go from idea to manuscript while preserving your authenticity. Authentically Created provides community, resources, and connections to help you publish your book as an Indie Author. Our commitment is to cultivate a culture of collaboration, authenticity, integrity, and artistic expression, ensuring that every voice has the opportunity to be heard and celebrated.

Learn more at www.authenticallycreated.com

www.ingramcontent.com/pod-product-compliance
Lightning Source LLC
Chambersburg PA
CBHW071153130626
46553CB00004B/1635